Learn the Fundamental Principles for Your
Own Personal Achievement and Success

Learn the Fundamental Principles for Your Own Personal Achievement and Success

A Training Seminar Manual

Life Coaching Training Seminar Series

By

Paschal Bernard Assey

PARTRIDGE

To order additional copies of this book, contact
Toll Free 0800 990 914 (South Africa)
+44 20 3014 3997 (outside South Africa)
orders.africa@partridgepublishing.com

www.partridgepublishing.com/africa

Table of Contents

About the Author

Paschal B. Assey, the Author of this Training Seminar Manual has been extensively involved in Poverty Reduction Initiatives in Tanzania. He holds a Master's degree in Public Administration from the Carleton University, Ottawa, Canada.

After graduating with a Bachelor's degree in Economics at the University of Dar es salaam in 1985, he was employed as an economist at the Planning Commission of the Government of Tanzania. He has also been extensively involved in numerous major national programs. Among the key programs are: - i) the Social Dimensions of Adjustment (SDA), (a program which was supported by the United Nations Development Program (UNPD), focusing on measures to mitigate the adverse effects of the World Bank supported Adjustment programs of the 1980's and early 1990's), and ii) It's successor program titled Poverty Eradication Initiative Program, where he served as the National Coordinator for about 10 years.

He was also among the key individuals in the development of national policy documents to coordinate poverty reduction initiatives in Tanzania, including;- i) The National Poverty Eradication Strategy (NPES); ii) Poverty Reduction Strategy Paper (PRSP) for Tanzania; iii) Poverty and Welfare Monitoring Indicators for Tanzania; iv) The Poverty Monitoring Master Plan and v) The National Strategy for Growth and Reduction of Poverty -popularly known by its Kiswahili acronym MKUKUTA. He also participated in developing specific targeted programs like the Small Entrepreneurs Loan Facility (SELF), Tanzania Social Action Fund (TASAF), and the Program for Formalization of Property Rights. He was also among the Core Team members that developed the Millennium Challenge Account Program for Tanzania (MCA-T).

In his career he has served in different positions including i) Training Manager on Socially Sensitive Planning with the SDA program, ii) National Coordinator for the Poverty Eradication Initiatives Program, iii) Assistant Director in the Poverty Eradication Division (PED), iv) Acting Director of the PED, and v) Deputy Chief Executive Officer –MCA-T.

He decided to compile this training seminar manual to share his major life lessons mainly drawn from his experience, seminars he attended, and the teachings and knowledge gained from reading and listening tapes of world renowned writers and motivational speakers on the Science of Personal Achievement and success. Included in this manual therefore are:-

- The Author's 5 major lessons from his long term involvement on poverty reduction initiatives and general life experience,
- Brief narratives of a few selected 12 Gurus on self-help and personal achievement,
- The researched 17 Principles of personal achievement ever written by Dr. Napoleon Hill –one of the icons on the Science of Personal Achievement;
- 5 secrets of life that the Author would like all readers to draw their attention to, and
- The key traits that cut across all successful people.

1.0

Background

I have been asking myself for a long time -why life coaching is not usually taught in schools and colleges? And where do people learn these necessary skills? To-date I don't have a definite answer. It appears to me that people learn life skills through trial and error methods with many coaches, counselors, volunteers and actors some of whom are not that reliable. If the skills were taught anywhere (in schools, colleges and or workplaces I have gone through) I am afraid I did not get it. Yet deep inside every person there is an urge, a desire or a wish to be successful, live a good meaningful life and achieve the highest, fullest expression of oneself.

There is a lot of literature out there, from ages, which address the subject from different angles. And also there are numerous individuals and organizations that attempt to fill the vacuum, in their different capacities. This manual is one of those attempts hoping this particular one, and others to follow, will in my little capacity, contribute towards building a body of knowledge that can lead to a solid base for a formal training in schools and colleges.

In this background I have summarized what this manual is all about and shared my life lessons in the foreword and explained briefly why I decided to prepare this manual. I have also included some few introductory remarks as a way of setting the stage for the actual training seminars that will be organized based on this manual.

1.1   FOREWORD

You will most likely be surprised with the truth about achieving personal achievement and success. Many people think there is a hidden formulae that is revealed to a few chosen people. The naked truth about the Science of Personal Achievement is that it is something that every one of us can achieve as long as the principles are applied consistently; and the most amazing thing is that the principles are not new – they are basic fundamentals which have been studied, written and discussed by many people for a long time. When you are ready to receive the master key to your success you will find yourself asking, as I did to myself, why did I wait so long.

The Secret of creating wealth is simply by bringing value to the market –by offering something of "use value" to people. We all know that every person on earth, famous or infamous, poor or rich, young or old, man or woman, able bodied or disabled has the capacity to offer something useful to someone else. Even bringing a smile in someone else's face is something that people consider of value and you will be surprised by the number of people who make fortunes by making other people smile or laugh.

One of the biggest lessons of life that I have come to realize, almost too late, and which I would like to share with you in this manual, may on its face value appear like a paradox. BUT so many people have testified that it is true. "YOU WILL GET EVERYTHING YOU WANT IN LIFE IF YOU CAN MAKE OTHER PEOPLE GET WHAT THEY WANT." I know some people will question it; but let me assure you that the secret to your success lies in a deep sense and genuine focus on solving other people's problems and offering what they need most. Brian Tracy and Tony Robbins have argued consistently that to be successful "FIND A WAY TO DO FOR OTHERS MORE THAN ANYONE ELSE DOES. BECOME MORE VALUABLE! DO MORE! GIVE MORE! BECOME MORE RESOURCEFUL! SERVE MORE AND SHOW UP MORE OFTEN."

If you cannot sell your product or people seem to ignore the services you are offering, or in other words there is no effective demand to your products or services, know that they don't see an added value in what you are offering as compared to what they already have or obtainable elsewhere. The fact that a product you are selling and/or services being offered are not required should send you a signal (or is a message sent to you) that you need to be more innovative, creative and imaginative in adding value to yourself and the products and services you offer.

I have researched and studied quite extensively on the factors behind personal achievement and success and why the majority of the people fall into the trap of the vicious circle of poverty. Out of my curiosity and search for more knowledge and understanding I have learned five key lessons which I would like to share with you in this manual.

The first major lesson comes from my long and extensive involvement in poverty reduction initiatives at the national level. It's the realization that **you simply cannot eradicate someone's poverty from without. True poverty eradication initiatives must come from within an individual; -from a strong determination from within an individual (that enough is enough) for a change.** The strong determination will necessarily force an individual to mobilize all the efforts, including seeking support from others, in pursuit of a different path guided by a strong sense of purpose and a burning desire. Note that the basic ingredients needed include i) definite/specific and clear goals ii) a burning desire and a strong determination capable of carrying you through the endurance that is needed to reach your destiny; iii) continuous learning from your own experience and the experiences of others and making adjustments and revisions of your plans and strategies, on your way to your destiny; and iv) massive action and empowering belief on your capacity to reach your destined mission in life. The empowering belief will help to bring you back to your path at the point of desperation and temporary defeat and failure.

It is true that a conducive environment that offers opportunities for many and policies that ensure a fair play and even affirmative actions to the poor contribute to poverty reduction efforts, **but** the driving force must be from within an individual. In other words, I can confidently say without fear of contradiction that poverty will not and cannot be eradicated from the supply side; it must be demand driven otherwise the efforts will not be sustainable. This is perhaps the reason why the objective of eradicating poverty is so elusive to many; it demands individual efforts and particularly serious individual thinking, goals setting and action.

The second major lesson is the realization of the big fallacy of life that traps so many people both highly intelligent as well as normal ordinary people. **Many people believe that circumstances, surrounding environments, cultural backgrounds, past experiences and broad policies shape their lives.** People believe that their capacities and abilities are normally limited by these circumstances. As such they end up blaming the circumstances and holding them responsible for any failure in realizing their dreams. Because of these limiting beliefs many people give up thinking about their goals and planning for their lives. They resort to wondering without a strong sense of purpose which inevitably leads to frustration and desperate living.

I must admit that this lesson first came as a surprise to me. This is mainly because I truly believed that people are usually limited by circumstances. This is why I worked for almost ten years reviewing policies, developing systems to monitor poverty trends, developing national plans and strategies and specific national programs to create conducive environment for a broad based growth which would offer equal opportunities for all and hence contribute towards poverty eradication. I must admit that I almost ended up a bit frustrated with the disappointing little results on the ground and hence I learned the hard way this major lesson that **what counts most is not the circumstances but a strong determination, creativity and hard work of the individuals.**

Failure to realize that **circumstances do not really determine your destiny (and hence blaming them is useless and is normally used as a mere excuse for individual frustrations in life),** traps so many people from all walks of life. The fact that both successful people and failures are found in all circumstances and in all walks of life is sufficient to prove that the same circumstances cannot really be the determinants of your destiny. In fact the same circumstances face everyone but some people are able to cope and others succumb to those forces outside them. The question is, why is it that others manage to cope with whatever limiting forces outside them and others fail? And can those who fail also be able to empower themselves and manage those forces? My research tells me that indeed those who fail can also learn the same tricks and manage their circumstances.

Hence there must be something else that explains the differences in the lives of different people. In fact the major limiting factor is the belief and the story we have developed which end up eroding our self-confidence and self-esteem. The truth of the matter is, if you truly believe so (that you are limited by your circumstances) then you already have sufficient reasons not to try hard enough and the results are predictable -that you will fail to do what you wished to do. **"As you think so it shall be".** The thing to remember is that, the moment you allow those thoughts, is the time you have already decided to fail because you won't do what it takes to accomplish what you wished to do.

But why so many people fall into this trap? The main reason is that life teaches us to find reasons for failure to avoid bad feelings (by nature people feel bad when they fail). And our conscious mind knows the trick to find reasons for anything –i.e. by generalizing situations. I have come to realize that with generalizations there are numerous reasons for almost anything! So to avoid feeling bad about yourself, for any failure, the mind starts looking at the environment surrounding you and your particular circumstances including your past history and compile a list of potential limitations which can hinder your progress and hence link them to your actions or inactions. To be able to avoid this tendency we should keep at the back of our minds that failure is a failure no matter how justifiable one can make it. The only good thing about failure is the learning experience we benefit from such occurrences.

The good news is that the limiting beliefs and stories we tell ourselves can be changed through a right mental attitude and empowering pattern of behavior. In this manual we will review the basic principles for personal achievement; we will also learn how to overcome the tendency to blame circumstances and finding excuses. By learning the principles and avoiding the tendency to blame circumstances and finding excuses, we will be able to take full responsibility of our lives and develop the right mental attitude that will guarantee our personal achievement and success.

The third major lesson is **the importance of driving ourselves at all times and not allowing anything else to control our mental attitude.** We must understand that if you are not driving yourself, or in other words, if you are not in full control of your mind, then you have automatically allowed (whether consciously or not) the circumstances to drive you and take control of your path to your destiny in life. You must also understand that there are benefits for taking full control of your mind and at the same time there are penalties that you must suffer for not taking full control of your mind. Some of the benefits for taking full control of your mind include sound health, peace of mind, decisiveness, freedom from fear and worry, positive mental attitude, personal fulfillment and joy. The penalties you must suffer if you neglect to take control of your mind include ill health, fear and worry, indecision and doubt, frustration and discouragement, negative thinking, resentment, anger and bitterness, jealousy, feelings of victimization, embarrassment and other emotional tortures.

It is a well-known fact that nature does not allow vacuum. So, if you somehow feel, you are not responsible for anything that is happening in your life you must be aware that you are, at the same time, admitting that there are other forces outside you that are controlling your mind and your life. If you happen to feel this way my message to you is "YOUR LIFE IS TOO PRECIOUS AND TOO SHORT TO ALLOW ANY OTHER FORCE APART FROM YOU TO DRIVE IT". Strive to take full control of your life and take full responsibility of everything that is happening in your life and enjoy your life.

The sad story and which I find to be unfortunate is the observation that the majority of the people allow to be driven by outside forces and hence go through life wondering, from this and that, without any definite major purpose. In other words they allow circumstances to drift them to no particular direction. The majority of the people therefore end up with some form of frustration and feelings of hopelessness, blaming those circumstances.

If you want to drive yourself you must realize that it is only people with goals who really know where they are heading. So if you want to drive yourself you must set goals and also learn how to become a goal achiever rather than a mere goal setter. This is one of the most important traits that you will have to learn and practice to become successful. This manual will prove to you that this is the most important distinguishing factor between successful people and failures. You will also realize that successful people are:- i) driven by a strong sense of purpose and mission in life, ii) set goals, write them down and review them regularly, iii) develop strategies and plans to lead them to their mission and goals and also review them often and make adjustments as needed to adapt to changing circumstances iv) develop personal and work habits and daily routines that propel them to their mission, v) avoid limiting beliefs and discouragements and instead cultivate empowering beliefs and the "can do spirit" which help to keep them motivated and capable of overcoming any defeats and temporary failures they encounter on their way to their mission and vi) they always have a strong reason which is beyond themselves that not only help them to keep their momentum but also help to avoid feeling complacent with their progress.

There is ample evidence to prove that people who become successful learn, early on, to avoid blames and looking for reasons and excuses for failures. They strive at all times to take full responsibility of everything that happens in their lives. All of the 17 principles of personal achievement explained in this manual amplify this lesson.

The fourth major lesson is that if you want to be really successful **your definite major purpose or your burning desire MUST NOT REDOUND TO YOU**. I started with this lesson at the outset because I found it to be so profound and yet so few people are really able to fully comprehend it. The majority of people (including myself at the beginning) never really understand this. In fact, to many people, this is a paradox. People tend to think "either or" -that is "you are either focusing on other people's benefits or your benefits" but not both at the same time. In this way people would tend to consider the focus on others as mere manipulation for individual benefits which renders the objective not to be genuine. It is important to understand that your focus on others **must be genuine** otherwise people will realize very soon if your interest on others is manipulative. An example of a product or a service in the market might bring more clarity to this lesson. As I pointed out earlier it is only when your product or service is genuinely focusing on the needs, tastes and market requirements that people will find the added value of your product or service. And when people find added value in your product or service they will buy more of it and end up earning you a fortune. It is that simple and yet difficult to understand.

The other realization related to this lesson is the fact that by nature people never really perceive full and long term satisfaction with whatever they accomplish for themselves be it riches, mansions, fame and respect. As such people always look beyond what they already have no matter what! Otherwise life starts to become boring when you start to feel that there is nothing more left to aspire for. As such, when living in abundance, you can only continue to be inspired by your goal only if it is beyond your personal needs and satisfaction. This means that your definite major purpose must be a goal beyond your personal needs and satisfaction; it must aim to benefit other people and the society or community around you; aim to contribute something to people's lives and human progress in general. Several writers have numerous quotes related to this including "ENJOYABLE SUCCESS IS SHARED SUCCESS.

So whether you go by human nature or by the market value logic, the conclusion is the same -"YOUR GOALS FOR PERSONAL ACHIEVEMENT AND SUCCESS MUST NOT BE SELFISHLY FOCUSED ON YOU". This is why it is indeed true that **"you will get everything you want in life if you can make other people get what they want";** what a lesson for your prosperity and success!!

The fifth major lesson is the realization that **only about 20% or so of your success comes from your knowledge, skills and experience (mechanical); the largest percent, about 80%, comes from your philosophy and psychology.** I must admit that I don't have a scientific proof of this assertion nor any scientific analysis that provides hard evidence on this. Frankly, this lesson also came as a little surprise to me because I tended to believe, as many people do, that hard work accounts for a greater portion of our successes.

I first got this lesson from Anthony Robbins seminar tapes and as I continued to listen and watch his videos and those of others like Earl Nightingale and Jim Rohn and read their books and particularly the "unlimited power" and "Awaken the Giant within" by Tony Robbins, I became convinced that it holds water and hence would like to share it with you in this manual. The above mentioned teachings and literature have strong and convincing arguments that your value at the market place (in society) is predominantly determined by your philosophy, leadership ability and perceived traits and not your academic qualifications, skills and individual experience. This is also what explains the remunerative differences between 2 or more people, with the same qualifications, skills and experiences, working in a similar environment, doing similar jobs/businesses. The reason your philosophy is more important than your actions is because it influences people and hence determines your leadership status in the society and the resultant payoffs that go with it. Your philosophy and psychology is also what motivates and empowers you. BUT at the same time it is important to be aware that your philosophy could also demobilize and disempower you. And this is what makes a major difference between people – **whether you have empowering or disempowering philosophy.** The reason why it makes such a huge difference between people is mainly because without empowering philosophy your **self-confidence goes down** and you also **lose your self-esteem** –the two traits which are absolutely essential for your success.

1.2   WHY THIS TRAINING SEMINAR MANUAL

This is a training seminar manual to inspire people to take full control of their minds and develop the right mental attitude that will guarantee them personal achievement / success in life.

> ➢ I am convinced beyond reasonable doubt that everyone, without an exception, can achieve success in life irrespective of the individual circumstances, the surrounding environment, gender, cultural and religious background, academic achievement or even individual intellectual capacity.
> ➢ At one point in our lives we all have had some good dreams and hopes for a bright future and envisioned

the kind of things we would like to accomplish in our lives. For many the dreams have fade away and instead a sense of hopelessness has creeped in and some have even despaired, leading very desperate lives.

➢ This manual is intended to bring back the hope and motivate you to keep moving in the direction of your choice and I hope it will bring back the lost hopes and your dreams for good life and hence get you back to your right path for your destiny. AND IT ALL STARTS WITH THE NEW WAY YOU WILL START TO THINK -FOR OUR THOUGHTS TRUELLY CREATE OUR RELITIES OF LIFE.

➢ Some observations:
  o It is only less than 5% of the population worldwide reach at the top of their desires and live in abundance—i.e. become fully satisfied with their personal achievement
  o About 95 % end up with some form of frustration, blaming everything else, but themselves, for their failures.

➢ Based on the lessons from my long term research, observations and readings I have decided to prepare this Training seminar manual on the Science of Personal Achievement and success with three main objectives in mind:-
  o To create a deep sense of awareness and appreciation of the distinguishing factors for success and failure and how people can cope with disempowering thought patterns and beliefs.
  o To help you to determine your destiny and develop goals and plans towards it and nurture a strong sense of purpose and a burning desire capable of propelling you through to your chosen destination.

- To help you develop the right mental attitude and discipline that is necessary to keep your momentum, overcome any obstacles you will certainly face on your way, and guarantee you success.

- This training seminar manual is intended to prepare you psychologically to be among the 5% of the population. – As pointed out earlier, please note that it's only 20% of your personal achievement is mechanical (depending on your skills, knowledge and experience). About 80% depends on your philosophy and psychology.

1.3   INTRODUCTORY REMARKS

These introductory remarks set a tone for the entire manual. It briefly explains the theme of this manual, what the manual intends to accomplish and how every one of us can accomplish whatever goals we set for ourselves by developing a burning desire for them.

- I did quite an extensive research on poverty while I was in the Poverty Eradication Division (Vice President's Office) for more than 10 years (1995 – 2005). One of the major personal observation was that "YOU CANNOT ERADICATE POVERTY FROM WITHOUT/OUTSIDE". Poverty eradication is not supply driven but demand driven. I learnt that **"THE MAJOR KEY TO YOUR BETTER FUTURE IS YOU"**
- I have read numerous books on the science of personal achievement and success. I have listened to renowned motivational speakers like Andrew Carnegie, Napoleon Hill, Wayne Dyer, Jim Ron, Jack Canfield, Leslie Brown, Brian Tracy, Bob Proctor, Nick Vujicic, Joseph Murphy, Earl Nightingale, Robert Kiyosaki, John Assaraf, Zig

Ziglar, Lisa Nichols, Anthony Robbins and many others. I have also read a number of inspirational books like "AWAKEN THE GIANT WITHIN" and "UNLIMITED POWER by Anthony Robbins. Based on those readings and tapes by motivational speakers, I believe that the major key to your success is you. Every person has a big potential for big achievements, prosperity and success in life. All you need is to stimulate it and achieve wonders. (If you really want to prove this, beyond reasonable doubt, listen/watch an inspirational video by Nick Vujicic titled "OVERCOMING HOPELESSNESS"). Yet very few people even bother to explore their potentials, let alone using it.

- What is apparently observed is that many people struggle throughout life without achieving much. Others work so hard throughout life and accomplish so little to the extent that life to them appears to be meaningless.

- Yet there are a few people who do not appear to be working so hard and using much energy but accomplish a lot, accumulate riches and are seen to enjoy life and everything appears to be working positively for them. People say "EVERYTHING THEY TOUCH TURNS TO GOLD"

- The big question is WHY? -This manual is about the why question, and what can be done to turn things around when life is not producing the results we desire. After reading this manual carefully, you will realize that hard work alone cannot guarantee you success. It must be combined with creative thinking, a strong sense of purpose and a strong belief in your capacity to accomplish whatever you have set for yourself.

If you would like to ignore everything else in this manual, don't ignore this One major lesson: Mr. Jim Rohn puts it this way: -**"life is not designed to give you what you need –It is programmed to give you what you deserve."** And Earl Nightingale noted **"your rewards in life are in direct proportion to your contribution – your services".** He continued **"if you think you can enrich yourself by deluding others you can only end up deluding yourself".**

- Are there success factors or failure factors that can be attributed to the results we get?
  - o I can certainly say YES! There are success factors and failure factors;
  - o This manual explores them and sets a path to your personal achievement.

- In fact **personal achievement is science** and from what I learned in Schools and colleges, science will always give you predictable results. There are specific principles which will guarantee your personal achievement/success, if you allow yourself to apply them consistently. -This manual will explore the principles and I would like to assure you that they were drawn from an extensive research and have been observed to produce similar results for all those who chose to apply them consistently.
- In this manual we will discuss the 17 Principles researched and elaborated by Dr. Napoleon Hill way back in the early 1900s. To date the Principles are still very relevant and valid. In fact Andrew Carnegie (Dr. Hill's mentor) wondered why people continue to achieve success through trial and error methods while the principles are clear cut and known for many years. And Earl Nightingale calls it the strangest secret of life.

Given the objectives of this manual and the introductory remarks above, I understand that some of you who have set goals before and failed to accomplish much, may start to ask yourselves what is the magic that this manual will bring to change your past experience and beliefs. I can say right away that the manual does not purport to have any magic formula to bring a miracle to you. I however strongly believe that if you decide to pay attention and digest the content, as you continue to read the manual, you might start to think and view goals setting and the whole philosophy about personal achievement and success differently. One of my mentors, Dr. Wayne Dyer once said "If you change the way you look and think about something the thing you look at changes".

I believe this manual will give you a new lens of looking and thinking about personal achievement and success. This is my main motivation for preparing this training seminar manual – the hope that it will positively change the way you have been viewing and thinking about personal achievement and success. To sum up, my motivation for preparing this manual is grounded on the positive affirmations from those who applied the contents of this manual, the observable results of consistently applying the principles and the assurance that success principles are universal, that is to say, they work for anyone who would choose to apply them consistently irrespective of age, sex, religious background, surrounding environment and circumstances.

This is neither an analytical book nor a document to try to prove something. It is a guidance manual or your companion towards your personal achievement. So read it as many times as possible and keep coming back to it for inspiration as you endure your journey of life. I believe this manual is packed with some good stuff and I hope you will enjoy reading it.

Some Provocative Questions:

i. Do you really believe that everyone can achieve success in life?

ii. Is poverty a good or a bad thing? (There are some people who strongly believe in the nobility of poverty but the reality is that poverty is very devastating).

iii. If everyone can achieve success how come that so few people really achieve it?

iv. Are there principles of success which are applicable by everyone or there is only a hidden magic formula which is only revealed to a chosen few people?

v. If there are principles of success and the principles are universal why do so many people decide to ignore them? (This question will reveal to you what Earl Nightingale calls the strangest secret in the world. –"We become what we think about." In other words we become the burning desire and goals we plant in our minds).

2.0

A Brief Overview of Some Selected Motivational Writers and Speakers

These are people who have researched extensively on the principles and the empowering philosophy and psychology for personal achievement and success in life. The following is what the selected few have observed and shared with other people in their seminars, workshops, motivational talks, and writings:

2.1   Napoleon Hill (1883 – 1970):

Napoleon Hill came from a poor family and without strong formal education. In fact when he was identified by Andrew Carnegie to develop the principles of personal achievement, he was astonished, thinking he was not the right person to do that. But he turned out to become the founder of the science of success which was built on his 20 years long research that led to the establishment of the 17 principles of personal achievement. He devoted much of his time studying the common features of the 20th century's greatest achievers. His exhaustive research proved that the essence of success lies within the 17 simple principles that when used together, serve as an infallible formula for achievement, that empowers you to convert any adversity into advantage, AND IT ALL STARTS WITH A THOUGHT.

- He is considered to have influenced more people into success than any other person in history;
- Many of the modern motivational speakers and writers draw heavily from Dr. Hill's work;
- He interviewed more than 500 wealthiest People in America at his time including his mentor and inspirational figure – Andrew Carnegie, and published a classic book titled "THINK AND GROW RICH" in 1937 which explained the landmark 17 principles of personal achievement. To date Bop Proctor one of the highest ranked motivational speakers in the world, and many others, still have the original version of this book; -They keep it as a treasure.
- He claims that the turning point in his life was the revelation by Andrew Carnegie and his deep acceptance that "WHATEVER THE MIND CAN CONCEIVE AND BELIEVE IT CAN ACHIEVE"
- He spent the rest of his adult life conducting seminars/ lectures/ workshops on the Science of Personal achievement and success.
- With Napoleon Hill's guidance you can achieve a level of mental self-mastery that will enable you to consistently:-
  - Overcome fears to reach your achievements;
  - Maintain self-discipline and self-confidence;
  - Develop strong personal initiative; and
  - Focus your thoughts into clear plans of action

Some quotes from Dr. Hill

-"Before us lie 2 paths –Honesty and Dishonesty. The shortsighted embark on the dishonesty path; the wise on the honest path; for the wise know the truth that in helping others we help ourselves; and in hurting others we hurt ourselves. Character overshadows money, and trust rises above fame. Honesty is still the best policy"

- "Every adversity, every failure, every heartache carries with it a seed of an equal or greater benefit"

-"Hold a picture of yourself long and steadily enough in your mind's eye and you will be drawn towards it"

-"Self- discipline begins with the mastery of your thoughts. If you don't control what you think you cannot control what you do. Simply self-discipline enables you to think first and act afterwards."

-"Most of us go through life as failures because we are waiting for the right time to start doing something worthwhile. Do not wait. The time will never be "just right". Start where you stand and work with whatever tools you may have at your command and better tools will be found as you go along."

2.2   Andrew Carnegie (1835 – 1919)

A self-made steel tycoon and one of the wealthiest 19th C. US businessman and philanthropist. Although he had little formal education, Carnegie grew up in a family that believed in the importance of books and learning.

- He was a self-made multi-millionaire and one of the wealthiest people in the world who started from the scratch, coming from a poor family;
- He accumulated much wealth during the first half of his life and gave it all away to charity during the second half of his life.
- He strongly believed that any person has the potential to accomplish anything that he/she desires and focus his/her mind on, as the principles of success are clear cut.
- Most of the 17 principles of personal achievement compiled by Dr. Hill are based on Andrew Carnegie's philosophy and experience.
- He was the mentor and role model for Napoleon Hill
- He strongly believed in the power of concentration and the need to directing people's mind, energy and belief into their desires. He believed that with a combination of these attributes nothing can stop you.

Some of his quotable quotes:

-"People who are unable to motivate themselves must be content with mediocrity no matter how impressive their other talents."

-"If you want to be happy set a goal that commands your thought, liberates your energy, and inspires your hopes."

-"A man who acquires the ability to take full possession of his/her own mind may take possession of anything else to which S/he is justly entitled."

-"He that cannot reason is a fool. He that will not is a bigot. He that dares not is a slave."

-"it marks a big step in your development when you come to realize that other people can help you do a better job than you could do alone."

-"All human beings can alter their lives by altering their attitudes."

-"Success is getting what you want. Happiness is wanting what you get."

-"No man will make a great leader who wants to do it himself or to get all the credit for doing it."

-"Concentrate your energies, your thoughts and your capital...the wise man puts all his eggs in one basket and watches the basket."

2.3   Brian Tracy (Born 1944)

Brian Tracy comes from a poor family but became an accomplished self-development author and motivational speaker. He has researched and written more than 45 bestselling books that have been translated in dozens of languages. He is the Chairman and CEO of Brain Tracy International, a Co. specializing in training and development of individuals and organizations and is a superstar and an inspiring speaker on personal success.

Brian Tracy is a self-made millionaire who learned his lessons the hard way. He left school before graduating and worked as a laborer for several years. He washed dishes, stacked lumber, dug wells, worked in factories and stacked hay bales on farms and ranches. He however was able to turn his life around, went to college and earned a Master's degree in administration and management from Columbia

Pacific University and in 1981 he began teaching his success principles in talks and seminars around the world

- Brian Tracy's top 11 Essential Tips for living a Successful life
  i) **Change your self-image:** -"the person we believe ourselves to be will always act in a manner consistent with our self-image" —"we will always tend to fulfil our own expectations of ourselves" —"Move out of your comfort zone. You can only grow if you are willing to feel awkward and uncomfortable when you try something new"
  ii) **Create helpful habits:** "Successful people are simply those with successful habits —they do the most productive things at any particular moment; they do one thing at a time and do the most productive things even when they don't feel like it.
  iii) **Focus on what is useful:** -"whatever you dwell on in the conscious grows in your experience" —"the key to success is to focus our conscious mind on things we desire not things we fear"
  iv) **Set clear goals. And write them down:** -"people with clear, written goals, accomplish far more in a shorter period of time than people without them could ever imagine"
  v) **Ask yourself helpful questions:** "after every difficulty, ask yourself two questions: -what did I do right? And —what would I do differently?
  vi) **Luck is predictable:** "If you want more luck, take more chances; be more active; show up more often"
  vii) **Focus on activities that bring you results:** "most people engage on activities that are tension-relieving rather than goal-achieving"

viii) **Realize that you have to pay the price:** "the price of success must be paid in full, in advance"

ix) **Keep going:** "Every great success is an accumulation of thousands of ordinary efforts that no one else sees or appreciates"

x) **Make a decision. Any decision. Just do something:** Decisiveness is a characteristic of high-performing men and women. Almost any decision is better than no decision at all"

xi) **Take responsibility for your life:** -"the happiest people in the world are those who feel absolutely terrific about themselves, and this is the natural outgrowth of accepting total responsibility for every part of their life" –"the more you like yourself, the better you perform in everything that you do" –"Disciplining yourself to do what you know is right and important, although difficult, is the high road to pride, self-esteem and personal satisfaction."

- He underscores the importance of habits for personal success quoting Aristotle that 95% of everything you do is a result of habits. He argues that all habits are learned and can also be unlearned.

Some of his Quotes:

-"Good habits are hard to form but easy to live with; bad habits are easy to form but hard to live with." –most of the time we develop habits by repetition".

-"Successful people are always looking for opportunities to help others. Unsuccessful people are always asking 'what's in it is for me'

-"You cannot control what happens to you, but you can control your attitude towards what happens to you; by controlling your attitude you will be mastering change rather than allowing change to master you."

-"It doesn't matter where you are coming from. All that matters is where you are going."

-"Develop an attitude of gratitude and give thanks to everything that happens to you knowing that every step forward is a step towards achieving something bigger and better than your current situation."

-"Look for the good in every person and every situation you will almost always find it."

-"I have found that luck is quite predictable. If you want more luck, take more chances, be more active, show up more often."

-"the act of taking the first step is what separates winners from losers."

-"the only real limitation on your abilities is the level of your desires. If you want it badly enough, there are no limits on what you can achieve."

-"you have within you right now, everything you need to deal with whatever the world can throw to you."

-"All successful people, men and women, are big dreamers. They imagine what the future could be, ideal in every respect, and then they work every day towards their distant vision, that goal or purpose."

2.4   Jack Canfield (born 1944)

Is a Harvard graduate with Masters in psychological education and one of the earliest champions of peak – performance, developing specific methodologies and results oriented activities to help people take on greater challenges and produce breakthrough results. He holds a Guinness book of world record for having 7 books simultaneous on the New York Times' Bestseller list.

- He has studied and reported wildly on what makes successful people different, what motivates them, what drives them and what inspires them.
- He is a strong believer and advocate of i) purposeful living, ii) positive focus iii) persistence and iv) continued action even in the midst of numerous failures.

Some of his important Quotes:

-"Successful people maintain a positive focus in life no matter what is going on around them. They stay focused on their past success rather than their past failures, and on the next action steps they need to take to get them closer to the fulfillment of their goals rather than all the other distractions that life presents to them."

-"Remember you and you alone are responsible for maintaining your energy. Give up blaming, complaining and excuse making and keep taking action in the direction of your goals –however mundane or lofty they may be."

-"There is no right reaction; there is only your reaction."

-"You only have control over three things in your life – the thoughts you think, the images you visualize, and the actions you take."

-"If you get clear on the what, the how will be taken care of."

-"Each day is an adventure in discovering the meaning of life. It is each little thing that you do – whether it be spending time with your friend, running a cross-country, meet or just simply staring at the crashing ocean –that hold the keys to discovering the meaning of life. I would rather be out there enjoying these things than pondering them. We may never real discover the meaning of life but the knowledge we gain in our quest to discover it is truly more valuable."

-"As you take a few minutes each day to quiet your mind, you will discover a nice benefit: your everyday ordinary life will begin to seem far more extraordinary. Little things that previously went unnoticed will begin to please you. You'll be more easily satisfied, and happier all around. Rather than focusing on what is wrong with your life, you'll find yourself thinking about and more fully enjoying what's right with your life. The world won't change but your perception of it will. You'll start to notice the little acts of kindness and caring from other people, rather than the negativity and anger."

2.5   Dr. Joseph Murphy (1898 -1981)

Dr. Murphy was a Minister Director of the Church of Divine Science for 28 years. He has taught, counselled and lectured all over the world and was an author of more than 30 best-selling books.

- • He was a world renowned authority on mysticism and mind dynamics. He remains a beacon of enlightenment and inspiration for many people who have attended his teachings;

- He teaches the simple, scientifically proven techniques and the astonishing facts about how your sub conscious powers can perform miracles to you (e.g. Healing, riches, friends, peace of mind). He asserts that prosperity, happiness and perfect health are yours when you use "the power of your subconscious mind"

- Dr. Murphy describes the 3 steps to success as i) find out the thing you love to do and do it, ii) specialize in some particular branch of work and strive to know more about it than anyone else, and iii) make sure the thing you want to do does not redound to your success only (bring to you only). Your desire must not be selfish; it must benefit humanity.

Some of his quotes:

-"The only path by which another person can upset you is through your own thought."

-"Busy your mind with the concepts of harmony, health, peace and goodwill and wonders will happen in your life."

-"The first thing to remember is the dual nature of your mind. The sub conscious mind is constantly amenable to the power of suggestion; furthermore the sub conscious mind has complete control of the functions, conditions and sensations of your body. Trust the subconscious mind to heal you. It made your body and it knows all of its processes and functions; it knows much more than your conscious mind about healing and restoring you to perfect balance."

-"The simple truth is that, it is never what a person says or does that affects him/her; it is the reaction to what is said or done that matters."

2.6   Robert Kiyosaki (born 1947)

He is an American investor, businessman, self-help author, motivational speaker, financial literary activist, financial commentator and a radio personality. Has written more than 15 best-selling books – his first and most famous book is the "Rich Dad Poor Dad". He argues that schools/formal education do not prepare people/individuals for life; -does not give them the necessary knowledge and tools for financial independence but to become the slave of their labour. He thinks there is no such a thing as a "safe and secure job". We must learn not to work for money but to let money work for us.

- He identifies the biggest problem being inadequate financial literacy. Many people cannot distinguish an asset from a liability.
- His definitions –Assets put money in your pocket and Liabilities take money out of your pocket.
- The rich accumulate assets, run businesses and make investments while the poor accumulate liabilities thinking that they are assets and live from hand to mouth.
- Compares the contrasting advices from his two Dads –one highly educated and a civil servant, biological father (referred to as the Poor Dad) and his best friend's father; not highly educated but was running several businesses and had lots of investments (referred to as the Rich Dad).

Some of his quotes:

-"The size of your success is measured by the strength of your desire, the size of your dream and how you handle disappointments on the way."

-"In school we learn that mistakes are bad and we are punished for making them. Yet if you look at the way humans are designed to learn, we learn by making mistakes. We learn to walk by falling down. If we never fell down we would never walk."

-"Winners are not afraid of losing. But losers are. Failure is part of the process of success. People who avoid failure also avoid success."

-"If you are the kind of person who has no guts, you just give up every time life pushes you. If you're that kind of person you'll live all your life playing safe, doing the right things, saving yourself for something that never happens. Then you die a boring old man."

-"the single most powerful asset we all have is our mind. If it is trained well, it can create enormous wealth."

-"The word "CAN'T" makes strong people weak, blinds people who can see, saddens happy people, turns brave people into cowards, robs a genius of his brilliance, causes rich people to think poorly, and limits the achievements of that great person living inside us all."

-"We all have tremendous potential, and we all are blessed with gifts. Yet, the one thing that holds us back is some degree of self-doubt. It is not so much the lack of technical information that holds us back, but more the lack of self- confidence."

2.7   Dr. Wayne Dyer (1940 – 2015)

Dr. Dyer is an internationally renowned author and speaker in the field of self-development and spiritual growth. He is the author of over 40 books including 20 New York Times best sellers. Despite his childhood spent in orphanages and foster homes, Dr. Dyer managed to overcome many obstacles to make his dream come true. He earned the fame as father of motivation in US.

- Through his early work in college teaching and clinical psychology he discovered the need to make the principles of self-discovery and personal growth accessible to wider audience.
- He is a strong believer in the power of thoughts. He argues "if you change the way you look at things the things you look at change."
- He further argues that the greatest secret of the universe which has now been proven by Quantum physics is "we literally create our reality/realities of life."
- He asserts that "You have the potential for anything you desire/think about."

Some quotes:

-"With everything that has happened to you, you can either feel sorry for yourself or treat what has happened as a gift. Everything is either an opportunity to grow or an obstacle to keep you from growing. You get to choose."

-"All blame is a waste of time. No matter how much fault you find in others and regardless of how much you blame them, it will not change you. The only thing blame does, is to keep the focus off you when you are looking for external reasons to explain your unhappiness or frustration. You may succeed in making others feel guilty about something by blaming them but you won't succeed in changing, whatever it is about you, that is making you unhappy."

-"You have everything you need for complete peace and total happiness right now."

-"The more you see yourself as what you'd like to become, and act as if what you want to become is already there, the more you will activate those dormant forces that will collaborate to transform your dream into your reality."

2.8   Anthony Robbins (Born 1960)

Tony Robbins grew up in a very poor family but turned his life around to become an entrepreneur, educator, a philanthropist, a motivational speaker and an author of several best-selling self-help books including the "the Unlimited Power" and "Awaken the Giant Within". He has worked with many public figures and is well known for his much-publicized "fire walk" seminars. Has coached several world leaders including George W. Bush, Bill Clinton, Mikhail Gorbachev and Princes Diana and also world top class athletes like Serena Williams.

- His books the "Unlimited Power" and "Awaken the Giant Within" will show you how to take control of your destiny (mental, emotional, physical and financial).
- He strongly believes that deep within each one of us lies a special gift. We all have a sleeping giant within us. A talent, a gift, our own bit of genius just waiting to be tapped. He argues that each individual has some unique features that distinguish him/her

from any other person but with equal opportunities for experiencing life to the fullest.

- The single most important lesson we can learn from Tony is that THE RESOURCES WE NEED TO TURN OUR DREAMS INTO REALITY ARE WITHIN US, MERELY WAITING FOR THE DAY WHEN WE DECIDE TO WAKE UP AND CLAIM OUR BIRTHRIGHT.
- He identifies three steps to create a lasting change; i) raise your standards, ii) change your limiting beliefs (this is critical – If you raise your standards but do not really believe that you can attain it you've already sabotaged yourself. You won't even try! You would be lacking that sense of certainty that allows you to tap the deepest capacity that is within you) iii) create quality relationships first with yourself by managing your emotions and then with others.
- Tony robins says that the greatest resource is relationships because it opens the doors to every resource you can think of.
- We also need to learn the skills for financial and time mastery.
- He asserts that "if you want to be successful you must stay committed to your decisions, that you will live your life at the highest level". Don't allow yourself to settle for something less than you can achieve, do, or want. BUT unfortunately many people settle for much less than they can do and have many excuses like parents, education, politics, government policies, school system, lack of opportunities, finances, circumstances, etc. All these excuses are nothing but B.S. (Belief Systems) which are not only limiting but are in effect destructive.

Some quotes:

-"what we can or cannot do, what we consider possible or impossible, is rarely a function of our true capability. It is more likely a function of our beliefs about who we are."

-"Beliefs have the power to create and the power to destroy. Human beings have the awesome ability to take any experience of our lives and create a meaning that disempowers them or one that literally save their lives."

-"Life is a gift which offers us the privilege, opportunity and responsibility to give something back by becoming more."

-"If you want to be successful find someone who has achieved the results you want and copy what they do and you will achieve the same results".

-"It is not what we once in while do that shapes our lives, but what we do consistently."

2.9   Earl Nightingale (1921 – 1989)

Earl Nightingale grew up in a broken family to become an American radio personality, writer, respected motivational speaker and a famous Author. In 1949, when he was 29, He was very much inspired by Dr. Napoleon Hill when he read his book "Think and Grow Rich". The book provided answers to the intriguing questions he had been asking himself including the question "How can a person, starting from scratch, who has no particular advantage in the world, reach the goals that he feels are important to him, and by so doing, make a major contribution to others?" He was very much enlightened by the 6 words he read in the book –Think and Grow Rich- namely "WE BECOME WHAT WE THINK

ABOUT". In 1956 he produced a spoken word recording titled "The Strangest Secret" which sold over a million copies making it the 1st spoken word recording to achieve "Gold Record" status.

- During his life time Nightingale wrote and recorded over 7,000 radio programs, 250 audio programs as well as television programs and videos.
- He was the author of the book "The Strangest Secret" which became one of the greatest motivational books of all time.
- He argues that we are what we are today as a result of the accumulation of thoughts that have gone through our minds. He asserts that we literally make ourselves through our thought patterns, but it is only the successful people who would admit it.

Some Quotes:

-"When you have an attitude of altitude, and when you are grateful for what you have, your chances to have a meaningful and successful life are greater. Start where you are now to develop this mindset. You have the potential to do many things, even those things you may think are impossible. Broaden your vision and keep moving forward – the sky truly is the limit."

-"Success is the progressive realization of a worthy goal or ideal."

-"To achieve happiness, we should make certain that we are never without and important goal."

-"The key that unlocks energy is 'desire'. It's also the key to a long and interesting life. If we expect to create any drive, any real force within ourselves, we have to get excited."

-"Without a goal we are much like the man with a boat and nowhere to go. Goals give us the drive and the energy we need to remain on track long enough for their accomplishment."

-"Don't take the attitude of waiting for people to be nice to you –be nice to them. Don't sit in front of a cold stove waiting for the heat. Put in the fuel. Act first."

-"Preparation for life is so important. Luck is what happens when preparedness meets opportunity. Opportunity is all around us. Are you prepared?"

-"Your rewards, all the years of your life, will be in precise proportion to your service. You are here to serve others, just as they serve you."

-"You are responsible for how your life turns out, and your attitude shapes that life for better or worse."

-"Work never killed anyone. It's worry that does the damage. And the worry would disappear if we'd just settle down and do the work."

2.10   Nick Vujicic (1982)

Nick Vujicic was born in Melbourne, Australia on 4th of December 1982, without arms and legs, otherwise with a healthy body. Initially, the Victoria state law prevented Nick from attending a mainstream school due to his physical disability, in spite of lack of mental impairment. However,

Nick became the first physically disabled students integrated into a mainstream school once those laws were changed. His lack of limbs made him a target for school bullies, and he fell into a severe depression. At age 8, he contemplated suicide and even tried to drown himself in his bathtub at age 10. His love for his parents prevented him from following through.

He also prayed very hard that God would give him arms and legs, and initially told God that, if his prayer remained unanswered, he would not praise him indefinitely. However, a key turning point in his faith came when his mother showed him a newspaper article about a man dealing with a severe disability which made him realize that he wasn't unique in his struggles, and hence began to embrace his lack of limbs. After this Nick realized his accomplishments could inspire others and became grateful for his life.

Nick gradually learned how to live a full life without limbs, adapting many of the daily skills limbed people accomplish without thinking. He is now married (with a wife and two sons), an accomplished world motivational speaker, best-selling Author (has written 4 books which have been translated in different languages) and an evangelist. Truly his life is a miracle.

- His key message is –NEVER GIVE UP until you succeed.
- Nick is truly inspirational. He gives a practical advice for realizing a life of fulfillment and happiness by building trust on others, developing supportive relationships, and gaining strength for the journey of life. He encourages people by showing how he learned to accept what he could not control, and focus instead on what he could.
- He is a true demonstration of the unlimited power within us that is nurtured in the power of thoughts and belief.

Some of his quotes:

-"I do believe that my life has no limits! I want you to feel the same about your life, no matter what your challenges may be."

-"I am gonna try again and again, because the moment I give up, is the moment I fail."

-"I never met a bitter person who was thankful. Or a thankful person who was bitter."

-"It's a lie to think you're not good enough. It's a lie to think you're not worth anything."

-"Along the way you might fall down, ...sometimes in life you might fall down and feel that you don't have the strength to get back up.....do you think you have hope? Because I tell you I am down here and I have no arms and no legs, ...it should be impossible for me to get up, but it's not!"

-"As long as I try there is a chance of getting up. It's not the end until you give up."

-"You have the choice to be angry with God for what you don't have or be thankful for what you do have."

2.11   John Assaraf (1961)

John Assaraf was born in Tel Aviv, Israel in 1961 but his family moved to Montreal Canada, when he was just 6 years old, where his father worked as a Taxi- driver. John had difficult time learning French and English languages and in school he was bullied and made fun of and a target of mischief-makers. His self- esteem plummeted and it became very difficult for him to make new friends and acquire the new skills he needed to progress in the new environment. Consequently he turned out to be a trouble maker spending a lot of time in the principal's office at school and receiving brutal beatings at home by his father.

When he was 19 his life changed. He broke away from his negative peers and family and left Montreal to live with his brother in Toronto Canada. While in Toronto he came under the wing of a successful businessman –Alan Brown, who inspired him to get into the real estate business and learn purposeful living and achieving success. It was at this point in John's life that he began to learn about the unbelievable power that reside in each person, along with the fantastic abilities of the human mind – the ability to establish any goals and objectives and then consciously achieve them.

- From troubled childhood and without family support, John Assaraf has become a serial entrepreneur, brain researcher, worldwide motivational speaker, Author of two New York times bestselling books ("The Answer" and "Having It All") and the CEO of PraxisNow and NeoroGym and founder of numerous high performing companies in internet software, real estate, life and business coaching, consulting and research of the brain.
- John's passion is discovering and teaching people how to release the mental blockages that hold them back from achieving their fullest potential.
- He believes and shows people and organizations how easy it can be to achieve what you want if you can unlock the mental limitations that we allow ourselves from our past life experiences.
- One of his most often quoted statements is that most people do a very good job in setting goals, but are really not very good at achieving them and

hence he teaches people how to become a goal achiever. He points out the mistakes that people make in setting and striving to achieve their goals and how to overcome them.

- He teaches that the people who are successful at anything never allow excuses, blames, reasons for failure and hence take full responsibility of their lives. He makes a distinction between being "interested in" and being "committed" to something; arguing that "if you are merely interested, you will only do what is convenient. You will always have reasons why you can't do what it takes to succeed."

Some quotes.

-"Do more of what you love, less of what you tolerate and none of what you hate."

-"Be very careful what you say to yourself because someone very important is listening....YOU!!"

-"The reason you have what you have is because that is what you have decided to settle for right now. Change your mind, change your life."

-"The most wonderful gift one human being can give to another, is in some way, to make that person's life a little bit better to live."

-"The most important part of living on your own terms and having it all is having faith and belief in yourself and in the intelligent power that created you."

-"Success tastes that much sweeter when you have people to share it with."

-"Here's the problem. Most people are thinking about what they don't want and they're wondering why it shows up over and over again."

-"If you do not master the art of self-discipline –you will succumb to the emotions and reality of regret."

2.12   Jim Rohn (Sept. 1930 – Dec. 2009)

Emanuel James Rohn (Jim Rohn) was born an only child and grew up on a farm, which the Rohn family owned and worked, in Caldwell, Idaho. He dropped out of college after one year thinking that he would be better off taking a salaried job to support his family. After dropping out of school, Rohn drifted and worked as a stock clerk for Sears which did not earn him much income and was upset and frustrated, finding it difficult to support himself and his family. It was this time that a friend invited Jim to a lecture given by the then Entrepreneur, John Earl Shoaff. Jim was instantly inspired by him and during the next five years, Shoeff tutored Rohn and taught him some of the simple yet vital life philosophies which he would go on to implement in his own life and later teach others. These philosophies were 'WORK HARDER ON YOURSELF THAN YOU DO ON YOUR JOB'; 'YOUR INCOME IS DIRECTLY RELATED TO YOUR PHILOSOPHY, NOT THE ECONOMY' and 'FOR THINGS TO CHANGE, YOU MUST CHANGE'. By this new outlook and approach to life Jim changed completely his life and started making a fortune.

After making his first fortune Jim decided to move, in the early 1960's, from his childhood home in Idaho to Beverly Hills in California. It was here where he was invited by a friend of the family to attend and tell his story at a local rotary club. This then began his legacy that would go on to outlive his life. Throughout the 1970's he presented seminars and began participating in self-development business called "Adventures in Achievement" which included both live seminars and workshops.

- Jim taught us that **success is simple and is the result of sticking to the basic**, but mostly missed, **fundamentals**. He always said, 'there are no new fundamentals. Truth is not new; it's old.
- Rohn is now recognized as a master personal-development trainer through his Seminars, teachings and books. He has written more than 25 books and audio and video programs. Some of his best-known works include '**Challenge to Succeed**' and '**The Art of Exceptional Living**'.
- Jim Rohn spoke to more than 6,000 audiences during his lifetime, personally teaching millions of people the fundamentals of success. Rohn emphasized the importance of **taking responsibility for personal growth**, and he taught people why and how to reach for a bigger, better, more vital life. He stressed the importance of personal development, not only to benefit oneself, but also those people whose lives we influence through our abundance.
- People like Brian Tracy, Jack Canfield, Anthony Robbins, Chris Widener, T Harv Eker, Mark Victor Hansen admit that they learned much from Jim Rohn.

Some of his Quotes:

-"Learn how to be happy with what you have while you pursue all that you want"

-"Profits are better than wages. Wages make you a living; profits make you a fortune"

-"If you want to be a leader who attracts quality people, the key is to become a person of quality yourself"

-"You cannot make progress without making decisions"

-"Formal education will make you a living; self-education will make you a fortune"

-"Days are expensive. When you spend a day you have one less day to spend. So make sure you spend each one wisely."

-"No one else 'makes us angry.' We make ourselves angry when we surrender control of our attitude."

-"One of the greatest gifts you can give to anyone is the gift of your attention."

-"You are the average of the five people you spend the most time with."

-"Discipline is the bridge between goals and accomplishment"

-"Motivation is what gets you started. Habit is what keeps you going"

-"Don't wish it was easier wish you were better. Don't wish for less problems wish for more skills. Don't wish for less challenges wish for more wisdom"

-"The challenge of leadership is to be strong, but not rude; be kind but not weak; be bold but not bully; be thoughtful but not lazy; be humble but not timid; be proud but not arrogant; have humor, but without folly."

-"If you really want to do something, you'll find a way. If you don't you'll find an excuse"

-"Happiness is not something you postpone for the future; it is something you design for the present."

-"We must all suffer one of two things: the pain of discipline or the pain of regret."

-"If you are willing to risk the unusual, you will have to settle for the ordinary"

-"If you don't design your own life plan, chances are you'll fall into someone else's plan. And guess what they have planned for you? –Not much!"

-"The worst thing one can do is not to try, to be aware of what one wants and not give in to it, to spend years in silent hurt wondering if something could have materialized – never knowing."

-"Success is nothing more than a few simple disciplines, practiced every day."

3.0

---

17 Principles of Personal Achievement

3.1   PREAMBLE

Many people have written about the principles of success. So there is a lot of literature, which is easily accessible in the internet. Given the volume of literature it's hard to think about a completely new thing that has not been written before. The literature obviously give differentiated versions of the basic things that can guarantee someone's success. However there are some common things that cut across when you examine the different writings. The key that opens the way to any individual success is what Earl Nightingale calls the "THE GOLD MINE BETWEEN OUR EARS" –THE WAY WE THINK. The basic ingredients to personal achievement therefore include **our thoughts**, the **decisions and choices** we make and **actions we take** consistently.

What has been confirmed by all the motivational writers and speakers is that **personal achievement or success in life is SCIENCE**. It is science because there are certain success principles which will yield similar and predictable results when they are applied consistently and effectively. But you may achieve everything that you planned to accomplish and still be unhappy because happiness comes from the feeling of satisfaction and self-fulfillment which is an art. Several writers have made a distinction between "The Science of Personal Achievement vs The Art of Self-Fulfillment".

There are 17 principles which were scientifically researched and proved by Dr. Napoleon Hill way back in late 19th C and early 20th C. In fact it is very difficult to find a contemporary writer/speaker on the philosophy and psychology of success and personal achievement, who does not borrow something from the work and teachings of Dr. Hill. He was inspired by Andrew Carnegie, the founder of American steel industry and one of the wealthiest people in America in early 1900s. Carnegie believed that if the principles of personal achievement/success were properly taught in schools and colleges, the entire education system would be revolutionized and would result far reaching impact.

Dr. Hill testified many times that his life changed completely and was able to change the lives of millions of people worldwide, after the realization of the Carnegie inspirational philosophy that **"WHATEVER THE MIND CAN CONCEIVE AND BELIEVE THE MIND CAN ACHIEVE".** This was a landmark discovery for Dr. Hill and he believed that it is the strangest secret of life which many people rarely fully comprehend. Dr. Earl Nightingale based on Dr. Hill's work, developed a Series called "The strangest secret in the world" where he asserts that **"We become what we think about".** He argues that all of us are self-made but only the successful people admit it! Leslie Brown drawing from Earl Nightingale argues **"most people fail in life not because they aim too high and miss –NO! But because they aim too low and get it."**

[Secret No. 1 of the manual: Except for natural things and life it-self, which no human mind can fully comprehend,

our minds create everything else. Everything you see today in the universe was once a thought in someone's mind]

Inspired by Andrew Carnegie, Dr. Hill interviewed more than 500 wealthiest people in America at that time, and documented the common things they were doing differently from many other ordinary people. It was a 20 years research work that culminated in the publication of an all-time best-selling book "THINK AND GROW RICH". He rightly boasts of creating more millionaires worldwide than anyone else through his Seminars, Workshops and Writings.

It is also important to note that **the principles** for personal achievement, if properly applied, **will yield similar results/outcomes irrespective of level of education, religious beliefs and background, cultural background, environmental conditions and individual circumstances.** If you learn and use consistently these inspiring 17 principles of success, you will learn **how to take full possession of your mind** (your gold mine) and your life, understand **how adversity can be turned to your advantage** and **develop harmonious relationships**.

3.2   THE PRINCIPLE OF DEFINITENESS OF PURPOSE:

This is the starting point of all personal achievement. **Without a definite major purpose you are as helpless as a ship in the middle of an ocean without a compass.** This is the distinguishing factor between successful people and failures. There is no way you can accomplish much in life if you don't have a strong purpose driving you. **The strong purpose coupled with faith and belief that it is doable will force you to set specific goals, develop plans and strategies, form rewarding habits that will keep your**

momentum and develop a strong rationale for whatever you want to accomplish.

Meaning:- Knowing exactly what you want in life and developing a burning desire, plans and strategies for its accomplishment.

What to Note (NB)

i) **Clarity** in your mind of what you want to accomplish. Napoleon Hill does not talk about mere purpose, goal, desire; he adds definiteness. Clarity of purpose helps to create a clear image and picture of what you want to achieve in your mind. A clear picture of what you want to accomplish is absolutely essential to enable you to overcome many distractions in life that could easily sway you outside your path to your destiny.

ii) You must develop **a burning desire** for what you want to accomplish. Mere hope is not good enough; you have to develop a strong determination so as to enable you to keep your momentum as you climb the hills and swim in the ocean of distractions you will most certainly face on your way.

iii) Understand from deep down that life has **no short cuts**. No one will bring to you sleeping your burning desire. You have to develop strategies and work hard (and really very hard) to accomplish your desire; but if your desire is really a burning desire you won't even notice the endurance you will have to suffer on your way. **Note this fact of life "LIFE IS NOT DESIGNED TO GIVE US WHAT WE NEED/ DESIRE; IT IS PROGRAMMED TO GIVE US WHAT WE DESERVE"**

iv) And guess what! You are **going to fail** several times but if you know exactly what you want and have managed to develop a burning desire and are determined to get it, you will never allow temporary defeats to stop you. You will get up after each failure and keep again going towards your goal. (Watch Nick Vujicic's video titled "OVERCOMING HOPELESSNESS" or "NEVER GIVE UP".

v) Your definite major purpose should **focus on improving the life of other people** and never solely on you. Never allow selfishness or be limited to goals that redound to you. **Note Zig Ziglar's observation of the secret of life "You will get everything you want if you can make other people get what they want"**

[Secret no 2 of the manual: To achieve big and lasting success never focus selfishly on your own personal benefits. Your central focus should be genuinely on other people's benefits]

Exercise:

-Take your time and determine what you want to accomplish in your life (Personal fulfillment, Professional, financial, health, spiritual, emotional, relationships)

-Decide when you want to achieve them –ie. Put some time frame to every goal you have set for yourself.

-Write down your goals in a clear, concise, positive manner and develop a habit of reviewing them daily and as more clarity develops adjust them to make them clearer in your mind.

3.3   THE MASTERMIND ALLIANCE PRINCIPLE

There is no a single individual who has ever achieved big or massive success without the help and cooperation of others. It is a well-known fact that two or more minds, working together in perfect harmony, accomplish much more than the total sum of each individual output. **The essence of this principle is that "No man can become a permanent success without taking others along with him".** You cannot achieve success in isolation.

Meaning:- A mastermind alliance consist of **two or more minds working actively together in perfect harmony** towards a common definite objective.

NB.

i)   **Don't strive to accomplish your major goal on your own**. Through a master mind alliance you can appropriate and use the full strength of the experiences, training and knowledge of others just as if they were your own. After all your major goal in your life **should never be selfish** – it must benefit other people too.

ii)   **Never attempt to manipulate others** –you should always strive to work in harmony, and be fair to everyone for sustenance of your alliance.

iii)   Always **think win –win.** It's only when you are thinking win –win that you can build the needed trust in the mastermind alliance principle.

iv)   Gather together **like minded individuals** in your alliance; otherwise it will become difficult to sustain the harmony needed for the principle to work effectively.

v)   Remember when you have a **true master mind alliance you can overcome almost any obstacle** you will face on your way.

Exercise:

Keeping in mind the steps for creating a Master Mind Group given below, list the people who can help you to reach the goals you set up under the definiteness of purpose principle:-

- Adopt a definite purpose with an objective to be attained by the alliance
- Determine the appropriate benefits each member may receive in return for his/her cooperation in the alliance and see that he/she gets them
- Establish a plan through which each member makes a definite contribution
- Ensure that harmony prevails in the group. Develop a team spirit
- Calculate the number of individuals in the group based on the nature of the purpose to be attained.

3.4   THE PRINCIPLE OF ATTRACTIVE OR PLEASING PERSONALITY

Without an attractive or pleasing personality you will simply chase your success away. A pleasant personality is key for a lasting master mind alliance and building a team spirit. The principle of positive mental attitude will be discussed separately but it important to note here that **it is almost impossible to develop an attractive personality with a negative mental attitude.**

Meaning:- Striving to develop a personality that every person would enjoy being around with, **a personality that motivates and inspires others**.

NB:

i) There are about 25 different **aspects of your personality** which you must strive to improve:-
- **Positive Mental Attitude (PMA)** -the right mental attitude is full of hope, optimism, generosity, integrity, courage, initiative, tolerance, tact, kindness, and good common sense.
- **Flexibility** – being able to adapt yourself quickly to changing circumstances.
- **Sincerity** of purpose
- Promptness of **decision**
- **Courtesy** –respecting other people's feelings under all circumstances
- Tone of voice
- The habit of **smiling**
- Facial expression
- Frankness of speech and manner
- A keen **sense of humor**
- **Faith** in infinite intelligence – fear of God
- A keen **sense of justice**
- Effective speech
- **Emotional control**
- alertness of interest –develop **interest on others** and the general interest of the world at large
- fondness of people and **humility** –avoid arrogance, vanity, egotism, give a good handshake
- etc

ii) **Avoid at all cost developing negative mentality** including negative emotions of fear, hatred, anger, greed, jealousy, revenge and superstitions. Instead strive to develop positive emotions of love, sex, hope, faith, sympathy, optimism, loyalty

iii) **Remember PMA is your most profitable asset** –and it is absolutely free! Your personality can be your greatest asset but it could also be your greatest liability -because it embraces everything you control – your mind, body and soul.

iv) Remember also -**to be happy make someone else happy!**

Exercise:

- list the elements of your personality in which you most need to make improvement
- what steps will you take to make these changes
- how will changing them help you reach your goals?

3.5   THE PRINCIPLE OF APPLIED FAITH

Faith is the dynamo of the science of personal achievement, the source of the energy to put your thoughts into action. It is a state of mind that must be cultivated to **empower you**. It is argued that the more you act on faith in infinite intelligence the more your mind will open to its power. And the more you see that power working in your life the easier it will be for you to act on faith.

Meaning:- Applied faith is **the mental attitude** we must cultivate and maintain before we are able to **take full possession of our mind.**

N.B.

i) Faith and belief system in general help you to keep going even when you are faced with temporary failures and defeat. **Faith keep you away from despairing**.

ii) Remember faith **can work both in a positive** way and get you all the benefits in life **and in a negative way** and get you what you don't want.

iii) Faith **enables you to take full possession of your mind** and if you don't control your mind you are allowing something else to control it.

 ➢ The **basic benefits of controlling your mind** are:- a) sound health b) peace of mind c) a labor of love of your own choice d) freedom from fear and worry e) PMA f) material riches of your own choice and quantity.

 ➢ The **penalties you will suffer if you neglect to take control of your mind**:- a) ill health b) fear and worry throughout your life c) indecision and doubt d) frustration and discouragement e) poverty f) all the negative emotions of fear, hatred, greed, anger, worry, superstitions, jealousy, revenge

iv) **All successful people have full control of their mind and use applied faith to mobilize their potential and keep their momentum**. But faith could be used in the reverse gear and produce undesirable outcomes. In fact the same **virtuous circle of success is the same as the vicious circle of poverty** depending on how faith is applied.

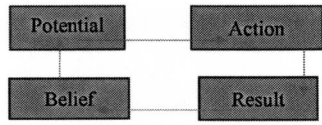

v) **Through faith you can demand anything you want in life**. Faith helps to mobilize your mind and direct it towards what you desire.

vi) In fact **your life is what you make it through your mental attitude**.

[The secret no 3 of the manual: Your realities of life literally come from your thoughts and the natural force that drives your reality is your faith or belief systems you have unconsciously created. If you didn't believe it; it will not materialize!!]

Lesson from Oprah Winfrey:

"You have to find a way to allow the truth you believe of yourself to come out! /manifest itself (to express itself)! You see "we are all looking for the highest, fullest expression of ourselves as human beings. And unless you do that you are not living your life!"

Exercise:

-What beliefs do you feel you must have faith in before you can reach your goal?

-Do you really believe you can do it if you believe you can?

-Is it true that a strong belief will never allow you to find reasons for failure no matter how many times you may have failed in the past?

- If you genuinely feel uncertain about the answers to these questions then you probably need to read "the Magic of Faith" by Dr. Joseph Murphy.

3.6   THE PRINCIPLE OF GOING THE EXTRA MILE

All successful people have this common and most important quality -they are **people of massive action**. They always tend to do more than what they are paid for and expected from them. They **love their work** and work very hard not thinking about the direct benefits they will get. **Usually they don't wait until they get a perfect plan before taking action**, instead they take action and perfect their plans and strategies as they gain more experience and learn more from their actions. **Successful people don't find reasons (do not allow reasons) for not doing what they need to do;** they will always find a way of overcoming the problems they encounter on the way and as such they will always go the extra mile; while **failures will always find the reasons for not doing** what they could have done and hence become frustrated and usually despair.

Meaning:- It is the habit of **rendering more and better services/products than you are paid for**; and taking personal initiative to ensure delivery of more services/products all the time **with a pleasing positive attitude** without expectations of increased pay (pro bono) or even distinguished recognition.

N.B.

i)   The quality of services you render and the quantity of services provided plus the mental attitude in which you render the services **(QQMA) determine the space you occupy in society and benefits you will get.**

ii)   There are numerous **benefits** of developing the habit of going the extra mile
   - Brings you to the attention of people who matter/ who can promote you
   - Makes you indispensable in your chosen occupation
   - Will enable you to write your own "price tag"

- Will improve your personality
- Helps to develop your imagination
- Inspires you to move towards your own initiative
- Keeps you free from fear of criticism by others
- Helps to avoid the disease of procrastination
- Helps to develop the definiteness of purpose
- Conditions your mind to maintain a Master Mind Alliance

iii) It has been observed that the **most successful people are those who serve greatest number of people**.

iv) You see –"that which **you share will multiply!** That which **you withhold will diminish!"**

Exercise:

- In your current job what extra miles might you consider going?
- To achieve your chosen goals what extra activities might push you faster towards the goals
- What might be the anticipated results of these extra efforts?

3.7   THE PRINCIPLE OF CONTROLLED ATTENTION

Successful people have the ability to **keep their minds on the things they want and off the things they don't want**. And because they are able to control their attention they can concentrate and **reap the benefits of concentration.** It seems a peculiar fact that it is easier to focus our attention on something that is not good for us than on something that is beneficial. This tendency is overcome when we learn to concentrate consciously. If you start practicing a few concentration exercises each day you will soon develop this wonderful power. **Success is assured when you are able to concentrate for you are then able to utilize for your good all constructive thoughts and shut out all the destructive ones.** You see -it is of the greatest value to be able to think only that which will be beneficial. **Theron Q. Dumont** in his book "The power of Concentration" argues **"Dwarfs can often do the work of Giants when they are transformed by the almost magic power of great mental concentration. But Giants will only do the work of Dwarfs when they lack this power."**

Meaning:- It is the art of **coordinating all the faculties of your mind** and directing their combined power **to a specific end**.

NB.

i) **Controlled attention is very powerful.** It harnesses many of the other principles, heightens their power and in turn concentration is enhanced. The more you **focus** your attention to something, the **clearer** it becomes.

ii) Forget the old saying "Don't put all of your eggs in one basket" in fact you have to **put all your eggs in one basket and concentrate your attention on protecting that basket and getting it to the market**.

iii) Concentration has been the hallmark of success for countless people and organizations.

iv) Concentration to your definite major purpose is essential. **It projects a clearer picture of your definite major purpose** upon your conscious mind and hold it there until it is taken over by your subconscious mind and acted upon.

Exercise:

Read the book titled "The power of Concentration" by Theron Q. Dumont

3.8   TEAM WORK OR THE PRINCIPLE OF COOPERATIVE EFFORT

This is related to the master mind alliance principle. The bottom line is the assertion that "until we become inspired with the spirit of team work and recognize the oneness of all people and fellowship of all humanity we will not truly benefit from the principle of cooperative effort." **Greed and selfishness will never lead you to success** and personal achievement. Paradoxically it is only when you are not selfishly focusing on the benefits of your work/actions/services that you benefit most. In other words "**you benefit most when you are focusing on other people's benefits** when taking an action or providing a service.

Meaning:- ability to inspire others and **build a team spirit** and maintain a commitment to the work you seek from others and for them to discover their own desires.

NB.

    i)   Remember that **individual effort is very limited**. There is no record of any great contribution to civilization without the cooperation of others.

    ii)   Remember also –most **people will respond more freely to a request than they will on order.** So you need to win people's interest/willingness; BUT **not** in a manipulative way because if you do it, they will soon realize it (something which will make them repel you).

iii) Note that –by **helping others** solve their problems you will also **help yourself** solve your own problems.

[Remember The Secret no. 2 of the manual: In fact personal opportunities/benefits are found in genuine initiatives to solve other people's problems].

Exercise:

- List some of your skills and knowledge that could benefit other people
- Think of the opportunities to use your skills, knowledge, experiences to solve problems faced by the community you live in/ or problems you observe that other people are facing.
- Figure out what it will take to solve the problems.

3.9 THE PRINCIPLE OF LEARNING FROM ADVERSITY AND DEFEAT

There are two important aspects of this principle that must be kept in mind. One is the fact that the circumstances of life are such that **everyone inevitably is overtaken by defeat**, in many different ways at one time or another. The other is the fact that **every adversity carries with it the seed of an equivalent benefit**. As such, it is important to realize that no one has attained success without experiencing some form of defeat. Hence you need **not accept defeat as a failure** but only as a temporary event that **may prove in the long run to be a blessing in disguise**. Realize that there is no limitation or defeat unless your mind accepts it so and allows you to consider it as a failure. It is true everyone at one point or another faces defeats, but **the event could be a stepping stone or a stumbling block, depending on the mental attitude it is faced**.

Meaning:- Any adversity or defeat that you suffer has a seed of an equivalent benefit that you can learn from. An **important part of the Science of Personal achievement is therefore to master the skill of looking for the seed of an equivalent benefit in every defeat** or adversity you experience.

NB.

i) Defeat should be accepted merely as a test which permits you to discover the nature of your thoughts and their relation to your definite major purpose. **You are never a failure until you accept defeat as permanent and quit trying harder**.

ii) Realize that **what matters most** is not an event that happens to you, or circumstances you find yourself in, but **your reaction** to the event or circumstances.

iii) Remember **in most cases adversities become your blessings in disguise**.

iv) 25 major causes of failure:-

➢ The habit of **drifting through life without a definite major purpose**

➢ Too much interest (**meddlesome curiosity**) in other people's affairs which do not concern you.

➢ Inadequate education

➢ Lack of self- discipline

➢ Lack of ambition

➢ Ill health that results from negative thinking and poor diet

➢ Unfavorable childhood influences

➢ Lack of persistence and follow-through

- ➢ **Negative mental attitude**
- ➢ Lack of emotional control
- ➢ The desire to get something for nothing
- ➢ **Failure to reach decisions promptly and firmly** when all the facts needed for the decision are available
- ➢ One or more of the basic 7 fears:- poverty, criticism, ill health, loss of love, old age, loss of liberty, death.
- ➢ Poor selection of a spouse
- ➢ **Over caution or the lack of caution**
- ➢ Poor choice of vocation or occupation
- ➢ Indiscriminate spending of time and money
- ➢ Lack of control over the tongue
- ➢ Intolerance
- ➢ Failure to cooperate with others in a spirit of harmony
- ➢ Disloyalty
- ➢ Lack of vision and imagination
- ➢ Egotism and vanity
- ➢ Desire for revenge
- ➢ Unwillingness to go the extra mile. ETC they are many!

v) Remember -defeats have benefits. The following are some of the benefits of defeat
   - ➢ Defeat **reveals and breaks bad habits**, releasing your energy for a fresh start with better habits
   - ➢ Defeat **supplants vanity and arrogance** (majivuno, kiburi) with humility, paving the way for more harmonious relationships
   - ➢ Defeat causes you to take inventory of your assets and liabilities both physical and spiritual
   - ➢ Defeat **strengthens your will power** by providing it with a challenge to greater effort.

vi) Remember –**fear, self-limitation and acceptance of your defeat** as final will cause you to "be bound in shallows" and miseries (Shakespeare) but these things **can be overcome by applied faith, PMA and definite major purpose**.

vii) If you accept defeat as an inspiration to try again with renewed confidence and determination, attaining success will be only a matter of time.

[The Secret No. 4 of the manual: It's the losers who are afraid to fail and yet they fail BIG. Successful people are never afraid to fail, they however learn from every single adversity and failure they encounter. Note that "As you decide to avoid failure by inaction you have already decided to avoid success"]

Exercise:

- Review your life both professional and in the personal realm and recall several obstacles that have stood in your way
- Think about those obstacles and what followed after encountering them
- Try to remember how many of them actually led to positive things; new knowledge, inspiration or a "lucky" break.
- Describe these incidents in detail.

3.10 THE PRINCIPLE OF CULTIVATING A CREATIVE VISION

This principle is related to the principle of taking personal initiative. It is the success principle which is **responsible for the building of all our plans and purposes**. It uses old ideas and established facts and reassembles them into new combinations and put them into new uses. It has been said that imagination is the **workshop where we fashion the purposes of our brain and the ideals of our soul**. Most successful people have learned the way to avoid "thinking inside the box" or "thinking within a bubble". Guided by their definite major purpose and a burning desire, most successful people let their imaginations run wild.

Meaning:- there **is always room for new ideas, imagination and opportunities** hence we must strive to expand our creativity and imagination. There is **no shortage of opportunities but limitation of imagination.**

NB.

i) There are **2 forms of imagination- synthetic and creative imagination**. Synthetic imagination consist of organizing existing ideas and concepts and facts in a new combination that gives you a refined thing while creative imagination involves complete new ideas and concepts. Usually **creative imagination has its base in the subconscious mind** of the brain (the 6th sense) and is the medium through which you recognize new ideas and newly learned facts; while **synthetic imagination springs from experience and reason**.

ii) Synthetic imagination recognizes limitations. Creative vision sees no limitations.

iii) Note that your imaginative faculty will become weak through inaction; and it can be revived through use.

iv) There is always room for new ideas. Likewise the **opportunities to become rich are unlimited**. Every problem out there is at the same time a business opportunity.

Exercise:

- Imagine your "ideal" life, the one in which your goal has been reached, things are the way that you want them, and you have everything you desire. What is that life like? Describe it in detail; what you have, where you live, who you love, how you feel.
- Imagine five alternative methods of achieving your goal; it's always good to have several choices. Let your imagination soar, held back by no barriers. Might these ideas be incorporated in your current plan?

3.11   THE PRINCIPLE OF SOUND HEALTH

Maintaining sound health is key to personal achievement/ success. **To maintain both physical and mental health you must avoid negative thinking, find time to relax, exercise, eat right and see a doctor when something goes wrong**. People who are keen to maintain sound health know that prevention is better than cure (treating diseases).

It is amazing to note the extent of contribution of **our belief systems** (we have created mostly unconsciously) to our health status. Many of the diseases that we suffer are psychological **(hypochondrial)** which means they can be cured through changing the thinking pattern and the belief systems. The **placebo effect** is a scientific proof of the power of belief in healing our bodies.

Meaning:- Striving to maintain a sound mental and physical health is an important component of the strategies for personal achievement and success.

N.B.

i) To maintain a **positive mental attitude** which is critical to maintaining sound health, you must conquer fear and anxiety

ii) Remember that anything **that affects your physical health also affects your mental health** and vice-versa

iii) **PMA is the most important quality for sound mental and physical health**

iv) Remember –**exercises** produce both physical and mental buoyancy. It clears sluggishness and dullness from body and mind

v) Eating well (Foods rich in minerals) and **balanced diet** (including fruits, vegetables, proteins, energy) helps to build the super immunity of your body.

Exercise:

- For one week keep track of everything you eat and drink. What % of that is healthy?
- Start taking note of the foods and drinks that could do you harm and do away with them.
- Start to exercise on a regular basis and notice how you feel after the exercises. Do you sleep better after exercises?
- Do you allow yourself to have sufficient sleeping?
- How could you change your life style or your schedule to incorporate a proper diet and sleeping regime?

3.12 THE PRINCIPLE OF BUDGETING TIME AND MONEY

Successful people **always care** about the **use of their time and money**. They all tend to find ways of avoiding wasting their time and also other peoples' time and money. They budget well their time and money. In fact you can easily predict what will happen in say ten year down the road by looking at the individual's time use and management and the expenditure pattern. Mismanagement of time and money is also very stressful and a major cause of stress related deaths.

Meaning:- Time and money are limited hence **must not be wasted**. They must be budgeted for personal achievement and success. **Don't waste your time and money and also don't waste other people's time and money.**

N.B.

i)   We each have **24 hours to manage every day**. The broad division of that time for an adult are:- 8 hours for sleeping; 8 hours for work; and 8 hours for private use and recreation. The major distinguishing factor between successful people and failures (doers and drifters) is how they **use their private time. While successful people use it to sharpen their skills, enhance themselves and open their boundaries; failures use it to sabotage/destroy/limit themselves**.

ii)   Like time, money should be spent **with a definite purpose in mind**. You must create a budget for all your expenditures and apply self-discipline to stick to it. Your income should be budgeted into **4 categories** a) food, clothing and household expenses b) health expenses including life insurance, c) savings and investments, and d) charity and recreation.

iii) To get things done don't waste ANY MORE time –DO IT NOW!

iv) Your attitude towards life determines your attitude towards time:

DOERS:

➢ Have a definite major purpose
➢ Manage circumstances and resources
➢ Examine every idea they encounter before they adopt or discard it
➢ Take risk and assume responsibility
➢ Learn from their mistakes
➢ Go the extra mile
➢ Control their habits
➢ Have PMA
➢ Apply faith in their own success
➢ Create master mind alliance to expand their knowledge and experiences
➢ Recognize their weaknesses and take steps to correct them

DRIFTERS:

➢ Have no goal in life
➢ Are controlled by circumstances and resources
➢ Hit from one idea about life to the another depending on fad or what they see /hear from TVs, Radios, Speakers/Orators
➢ Run from opportunity and blame others for their lots in life
➢ Make the same mistakes again and again
➢ Do only what it takes to get by
➢ Let their habits to control them
➢ Have negative mental attitude
➢ Never do much to improve their situation

> ➢ Spend too much time watching TVs
> ➢ Would not know a weakness if it bit them

v) Remember some mistakes can be corrected but not the mistake of wasting time. **When time is gone, it's gone forever**.

Exercise:

- Make a list of all things you need to do and divide them into i) important and urgent ii) important but not urgent iii) unimportant but urgent and iv) unimportant and not urgent
- Review the list every day and adjust as needed and allocate your time and money in the order of priority
- Build this into your habit.

3.13 THE PRINCIPLE OF TAKING PERSONAL INITIATIVE

This is another major factor that distinguishes successful people from failures / doers from drifters / active from passive people. **Achievers know that it is better to act on a plan that is still weak/imperfect than to wait too long trying to perfect the plan and not take action**. Procrastination is the arch-enemy of personal initiative.

Meaning:- It is the **inner power that starts all actions**. It refers to the inner force that helps you to take your imaginations, ideas and thoughts into action. **It is the force that changes dreamers to effective actors.**

N.B.

i)   Remember: your success is something that you will **achieve through your personal initiative**, without someone telling you what to do or how to do it. You will definitely learn from others but you will have to take personal initiative, learning from your models, to figure out how you want to achieve your success.

ii) The habit of taking personal initiative, not only **inspires one to move on his/her own definite major purpose and responsibilities** but also influences him/her **to follow through** until he/she has completed what was intended.

iii) Remember: A **winner never quits** and a **Quitter never wins**

iv) the **major attributes** of personal initiative include:-

➤ Will force you to **have a definite major purpose and a plan** to achieve it

➤ Will help you in **building the mastermind alliance** with people who can assist you in achieving your definite major purpose

➤ Will give the necessary **persistence** and the will to win and carry you along when the going becomes tough or when your meet obstacles

➤ Helps you to **make decisions promptly** when all the necessary facts are available and change them slowly if at all.

➤ Helps you to follow the habit of **doing more than you are paid for** and in a pleasing mental attitude

➤ Enable you to **accept full responsibility** for everything you undertake and **never blame others and circumstances** when things go wrong

➤ Enables you to **take friendly criticisms** without resentment

> ➤ Enables you to **concentrate your attention** on one thing at a time
> ➤ Helps you to have a **Positive Mental Attitude** at all times when in communication with other people
> ➤ Does not allow you to put for morrow what could have been done yesterday.

v) Remember: **procrastinators are experts in creating alibis**

3.14   THE PRINCIPLE OF MAINTAINING POSITIVE MENTAL ATTITUDE

A positive mental attitude is the single most important principle of the Science of success, without which you cannot get the maximum benefit from the other sixteen principles. And remember **your mental attitude is the only thing over which you, and only you, have a complete control**. A positive mental attitude **attracts opportunities** for success while a negative mental attitude repels opportunities and drives away people. **A positive mind finds a way it can be done... a negative mind looks for all the ways it can't be done.**

Meaning:- A positive mental attitude is the belief that one can increase his/her achievements through **optimistic thought processes**.

NB.

i) What you must do to keep your mind positive
  ➤ Learn to adjust yourself to other people's state of mind and difficulties and **get along** with

them peacefully and refrain from taking notice of trivial things and circumstances. **Great people always avoid small incidences of controversy whenever possible.**

➢ Establish for yourself a fixed **system of conditioning your mind at the beginning of each day** so you will keep it positive under all circumstances.

➢ Learn the **art of selling yourself to other people** by indirections such as asking leading questions which bring reaction you desire and do not permit yourself to be drawn into arguments over trivial things and unimportant subjects.

➢ Begin each day with **a good laughing** because it will change the chemistry of your brain and start you out with PMA.

➢ Start each day with an expression of **gratitude** for all your adversities, defeats and failures you have suffered in the past and search for a seed of equivalent benefit then give thanks to the blessings you expect to receive during the day.

➢ Learn to concentrate **attention to the "Can Do" portion** of your problems and start action where you stand.

[The Secret No. 5 of the manual: PMA attracts success and negative mental attitude drives away opportunities no matter how justified you may be in becoming negative. Dr. Dyer agues "there is no justified resentment"]

3.15   THE PRINCIPLE OF CONTROLLED ENTHUSIASM

Controlled enthusiasm helps you to progress steadily towards success just as gasoline acts in a car's engine. **It is the fuel that drives things forward.** It is closely related to INSPIRATION which is the power that can transform adversity, failure and temporary defeat into action. By controlling your enthusiasm you can change any negative expressions and experiences into positive ones. **Enthusiasm stimulates your subconscious mind.** By feeding your conscious mind with enthusiasm you **impress upon your subconscious that your burning desire, and your plan for attaining it, are certain.**

Meaning:- Enthusiasm is **a state of mind that inspires action** and is the most contagious of all emotions. It is **more powerful than logic, reason or rhetoric** in getting your ideas across and in winning over others to your viewpoint.

N.B.

i) Enthusiasm is **power. By controlling your enthusiasm, you can change any negative expressions and experiences, into positive ones.**

ii) Controlled enthusiasm has many **positive effects**:-
   - ➢ Can increase intensity of your thinking and imagination
   - ➢ Helps you to acquire a pleasing and convincing tone of voice
   - ➢ Reduces the drudgery in your work
   - ➢ Can enhance your attractive personality
   - ➢ Makes you gain more self confidence
   - ➢ Strengthens your mental and physical health
   - ➢ Builds your personal initiative
   - ➢ Helps to overcome physical and mental fatigue more easily
   - ➢ Can influence others easily

iii) However there are some **dangers of uncontrolled enthusiasm**

➢ Can lead to **monopolization of conversation** which makes others turn you off/ repel you
➢ Could also **cloud your judgement** -leading to inaccurate thinking
➢ Could also **divert your attention from the important things** you need to focus your attention on for your definite major purpose.

3.16   THE PRINCIPLE OF SELF - DISCIPLINE

Most people act first and think about the consequences later. Self-discipline helps you to reverse that process. **By exercising self-discipline you will learn to think before you act.** Earlier principles have placed heavy emphasis on the importance of taking control of your mind which is pivotal to your personal initiative, positive mental attitude and controlled enthusiasm. **Exercising self-disciple helps to tie them together and make you unstoppable.** Self-disciple is not only important for mastery of your negative habits but more particularly to the development and enforcement of positive habits and hence enabling you to reap the benefits of PMA. **You have to exercise self-discipline before you are able to embrace the great master key to riches.**

Meaning:- Self-discipline is **the process that ties together all of your efforts of controlling your mind**, **your personal initiative, positive mental attitude and your enthusiasm**

N.B.

i) Key areas where self- discipline is necessary to develop positive habits include:-

> Controlling your tongue by learning the habit of thinking first before you speak. **A loose tongue is most of the time a big liability**

> Controlling the tendency to hit back on those you have a cause, real or imaginary, for a grievance. You must remember that everything you do for or to others you do for yourself because every **thought you have about others comes back to you in kind**.

> Controlling your emotions and particularly the emotion of love, hate, fear and sex. These are the big four emotions that can **make** or **break** you according the extent of discipline you exercise on them.

> Controlling your **mental attitude at all times**. Lack of discipline on your mental attitude can and often does drive away friends, destroys opportunities, brings on physical and mental illness, develops stomach ulcers, and makes peace of mind impossible.

> Controlling your stomach through dieting and fasting

> Also you have to exercise self-discipline in relation to **religion and politics** because through-out life you **meet with people with varying beliefs and ideologies**.

> The most important area is to **discipline yourself to take possession of your mind** and directing it to whatever ends you may desire.

ii) Some of the **benefits of exercising self-discipline**:-
   ➢ No one becomes very **wise** without the aid of self-discipline
   ➢ Brings **peace of mind** and happiness
   ➢ Is the means of **transmuting sorrow to faith**
   ➢ Enable **PMA**

iii) Without self-discipline you are as dangerous as a car running downhill without brakes or steering wheel!!

3.17   THE PRINCIPLE OF ACCURATE THINKING

Successful people realize that they are what they think. They know that **thoughts have power** but also understand thoughts are **under your control** and can be used wisely and bring you success or unwisely and cause you misery and frustration. Accurate thinkers accept no political, religious or other type of thought, regardless of its source, until it is carefully analyzed and hence they are able to master their emotions. **Accurate thinking is the essence of controlling your mind and we know if you are not in full control of your mind then you are automatically, but unconsciously, allowing other people to control you and your emotions.**

Meaning:- ability to **base your thinking on facts and not opinions of others** and not allowing anybody to do the thinking for you.

N.B.

i) An accurate thinker recognizes all the facts of life both good and bad and **assumes responsibility** of separating and organizing the two, choosing those which serve his needs and rejecting all others.

ii) The rules of accurate thinking which all successful people follow are either based on inductive or deductive reasoning. **Inductive reasoning** is used when the basic facts on which to base your thinking are **not** available – in this case you act on hypothesis while **deductive reasoning** is used when all the facts to base your thinking are available.

iii) For accurate thinking you must determine whether you are dealing with important facts, unimportant facts, fiction or mere opinions.

iv) Remember **most opinions don't have much value** because they are based on biases, prejudice, intolerance, guesswork, hearsay evidence and outright ignorance. (This is what causes so many atrocities we see in life)

v) Note also that accurate thinkers are the **masters of their emotions**

vi) **The more successful the person is, the less He/she is inclined to express wild and unjustified opinions about anything.** You might have observed that drifters, who are usually full of frustrations, give statements of opinions about almost everything they can imagine of.

vii) Do **not allow anyone to think for you** or influence your thinking except by the rules of accurate thinking. The **7 rules for accurate thinking** are:-

- **Never accept any opinions of other people as facts until you have satisfied yourself about the sources of the facts** and their accuracy

- Remember that **free advice, no matter from which source it is received, is worth exactly what it costs.** It needs examination before it is acted upon as safe.

- **Alert yourself immediately when you hear someone discrediting or talking negatively**

about another person because most likely He/
she will be talking from bias, to say the least.

- When seeking information **do not disclose why
  you want the information** because most people
  will tend to bias the information being given to
  suite your purpose.
- **Remember anything that exists in the world
  is capable of proof** and where such proof is not
  available it is safer to assume nothing exists.
- Both truth and falsehood, no matter by what
  means they may be expressed carry with them a
  silent invisible means of identifying themselves
  as such.
- **Follow the habit of asking the question
  "HOW DO YOU KNOW?"** when anyone makes
  a statement you cannot identify as true.

Exercise:

- To appreciate the need for accurate thinking ponder
  about the fact that "you are what you think and believe"
- Read more literature about the power of thoughts
  and accurate thinking.

3.18   THE COSMIC HABIT FORCE PRINCIPLE

**It is the means by which everyone can put into operation
a power by which your aims and purposes are attained
almost automatically by the action of your habits.** It is
only the human being who is given power to use this law to
establish his/her own habits and determine his own desires
and purposes for life.

Meaning:- It is the law of nature which is the basis of all of our habits both good habits and bad habits. **It is the natural law that balances nature enabling seeds to grow to plants and trees, the sun to spin around the earth and cause days and nights in a consistent regular manner, fixes the life patterns of every living thing and controls the universe.**

N.B.

i) The **orderliness of the world** of natural laws gives evidence that they are under control of a universal plan

ii) Cosmic habit force give **animals and insects instincts** but **man can rise above instincts** (fixed patterns of life) and establish his own patterns.

iii) **This privilege is the only thing by which a human being has a complete power of control and direction**

iv) this law has **both negative and positive potential application:- the negative application is called hypnotic rhythm which means – by our neglect to fix our thoughts upon the things we desire in life and thereby gain the power of cosmic habit force in attaining these desires, the law automatically acts in the negative hypnotic rhythm and fixes our mind on things we do not desire and hence attracts to us the physical equivalent of those things.**

v) **Remember your mental attitude is something you have full control over.** You must use self-discipline until you create a thought pattern or thought habits which keep your mental attitude positive at all times. This is what makes you what you are where you are now.

[Remember the secret No.1 of this manual – our thoughts create our reality –in fact we literally create our own realities of life through the cosmic habit force].

3.19   THE SUMMARY OF THE PRINCIPLES

Looking at the 17 principles one can group them into the following **7 categories which then become the distinguishing features of all high performance / achievers**:-

1) The practice of **setting clear and definitive goals**, plans and strategies and growing a **strong desire/ passion to accomplish them**; In this category 3 of the 17 principles can be identified namely:-
   i. The principle of Definiteness of purpose
   ii. The principle of Creative vision –the power of visualization
   iii. The Principle of Budgeting time and money

2) The Habit of always striving to build good relations and cultivating a **team spirit and win – win attitude** in accomplishing your mission; In this category 2 of the 17 principles can be identified namely:-
   i. The mastermind alliance principle
   ii. The principle of inspiring team work

3) The drive to develop an **attractive personality** and nurturing the **right mental attitude**; In this category 2 of the 17 principles can be identified namely:-
   i. The principle of developing a pleasing personality
   ii. The principle of cultivating a Positive Mental attitude at all times

4) Recognition of the power of thoughts and hence ensuring full **control of the mind** and not allowing negative thoughts to de-rail us; In this category 4 of the 17 principles can be identified namely:-
   i.   The principle of self-discipline
   ii. The principle of accurate thinking
   iii. The principle of controlled attention
   iv. The principle of controlled enthusiasm

5) Recognition that **action is what counts** and **not** merely good ideas and imaginations; hence the need to develop the habit of taking swift and **massive action and not wait too long to perfect the plans;** i.e fighting procrastination; In this category 2 of the 17 principles can be identified namely:-
   i.   The habit of going the extra mile
   ii. The habit of taking personal initiative

6) Taking all measures to ensuring **sound health**; In this category 1 of the 17 principles can be identified namely:-
   i.   The principle of maintaining sound health

7) Recognition of the **power of self-confidence** and **the need to build self-empowering belief systems and applied faith** that would never allow you to accept temporary failures as final; and allowing yourself to despair; i.e. the habit of not accepting self-imposed limitations and succumbing to excuses and blaming. In other words taking full responsibility of your life. In this category 3 of the 17 principles can be identified namely:-
   i.   The principle of learning from adversity and defeat
   ii. The principle of applied faith
   iii. The principle of Taping from the Cosmic Habit Force

4.0

Dream Big and Determine to Live Your Dreams

4.1   PREAMBLE

In this section I have picked the principles of success as articulated by Brian Tracy who has also researched extensively on personal achievement and has written his own version of the principles of success. In essence his principles are not fundamentally different from the landmark 17 principles elaborated by Dr. Hill. They are summarized here just for your information and appreciation of their similarity.

Brian Tracy strongly believes that the average person has an enormous untapped potential. He argues that you can move ahead far faster towards your goals if you learn and practice the key methods, techniques and strategies used by other successful people. In his book the "The 21 Success Secrets of Self-Made Millionaires" he asserts that every person can become successful. Achieving success is not a matter of luck or accident or being at the right place at the right time. He outlined 21 Success principles which he strongly believes will guarantee anybody big success if they are consistently and persistently applied. He gives the assurance that nothing in the world is capable of stopping anyone who apply them.

This assurance stems from his philosophy that "we are the architects of our own destiny; the masters of our own fate". And that "there are no limitations to what you can do, have or be, except the limitations we place on ourselves by our own thinking".

4.2   THE SUCCESS PRINCIPLES BY BRIAN TRACY

The following is a summary of 21 Secrets of Success as outlined by Brian Tracy:-

i)   Dream big dreams:-
- All great men and women start with a dream and it remains the starting point for any meaningful achievement in life.
- Dreams make us more determined. They also inspire us and raise our self-esteem and self-confidence; -factors necessary for a better understanding and use of our unlimited potential.
- Many people never exploit their dreams and hence they never get started.

ii)   Develop a clear sense of direction:-
- Write down your goals, review them often and develop plans and strategies to accomplish your goals. Remember to adjust the plans and strategies as you gain more experience and also as circumstances change.
- Thinking how you can achieve your goals stimulates your mental capacity and creativity. Remember you become what you think about most of the time.
- Take massive action, starting today, towards your goals

iii) See yourself as self-employed for whatever you are doing:-
- Refuse to blame other people for whatever limitations you face towards your goals and consider yourself always in charge
- Self-employed people are usually results oriented, more motivated, inclined to volunteer and are always looking for more assignment/ work
- With this attitude you will most likely become a respectable employee in any organization.

iv) Do what you love to do:-
- Find out what you naturally enjoy doing; what you have a natural talent for and do it very well
- Find a job that you can totally be absorbed in
- The litmus test is "Will you continue to do what you are doing for free?"

v) Commit for excellence:-
- Resolve today to be the best at what you do. All successful people continuously strive to deliver excellent work wherever they are.
- Give yourself self-confidence that there is no one smarter or better than you on your occupation.
- Striving for excellence will make you feel terrific about yourself as it will climb you to the top of your field.

vi) Develop a workaholic mentality:-
- Start early, work harder and stay longer; and focus on output
- Don't allow to be distracted by other unimportant things at your work area

- Resolve to become the hardest working person in your area of work. This will definitely bring you to the attention of those who matter.

vii) Dedicate yourself to life-long learning;
- Your mind is like muscle, it develops as you train it.
- Successful people determine to continue learning and becoming better for the rest of their life.
- Read many books, watch inspirational videos and listen to audio programs

viii) Pay yourself first: resolve to always put 10% of your income in your special account
- Develop a lifelong habit and discipline yourself to make regular savings
- We normally buy many things which we don't use; learn to avoid this tendency and practice frugality.

ix) Learn every detail of your business
- There is no alternative; you simply have to understand your business very well.
- Get along with others in your business.
- Remember the market only pay excellent rewards to excellent services and average to average work/services.
- Remember also that one small detail can be the turning point in your career.

x) Dedicate yourself to serving others;
- All self-made millionaires have obsession with customer service
- Always keep asking yourself -how can I offer the best services? And what are the best services?
- Genuinely dedicate yourself to helping others
- Always look for opportunities to do more; go the extra mile.

xi) Be impeccably honest to yourself and others;
- Strive to build a reputation for integrity and never compromise it
- Set high standards for yourself
- Always strive to do what you consider to be the right thing at the moment

xii) Set priorities and concentrate on one thing at a time
- By setting priorities you can accomplish almost everything in life. Remember that this is one of the hardest thing to do by most people, so give yourself the level of discipline required
- Strive to focus on results and not the activities.
- Determine the most valuable way of using your time.

xiii) Develop a reputation for speed and dependability
- People who do things faster attract more opportunities and possibilities.
- Serve people as fast as you can. Move fast on anything you do

xiv) Be prepared to climb from peak to peak in your life and career
- But remember life has ups and downs
- Don't allow yourself to become emotionally demobilized for some short term ups and downs of daily life
- Learn to accept that life is two steps forward, one step back.
- Become confident and relaxed with short term fluctuations in life

xv) Practice self-disciple in all things
- Set goals and discipline yourself to stick to those things that lead to your goals

- Learn to practice self-control, self-mastery, self-direction
- Successful people train themselves to do things the failures don't like to do. They may not like them either but they discipline themselves to go beyond their comfort zones

xvi) Unlock your inborn creativity and curiosity
- Remember you are a potential genius
- It is true that you are smarter than you ever imagined
- Your capacity to succeed is unlimited
- Your creativity is like muscle. The more you use it the greater it enlarges

xvii) Get around the right people;
- Be more with the likeminded people and particularly positive people
- Avoid negative people and particularly people who complain, look for excuses, blame, look down/despise others.
- Remember that everything is actually about relationships. Associate with successful people
- Be more of a goal giver than a goal getter
- Always look for ways to help other people
- Rule of thumb: the more you help others without expectations of return the more rewards will come back to you from unexpected sources.

xviii) Take excellent care of your physical health
- Aim to reach 80, 90 years with excellent health
- Ask yourself if the way you are living today could enable you to live up to 90 years
- Maintain proper weight and diet; avoid sugars, salts, white flours; eat more vegetables, fruits; and also exercise regularly.

xix) Be decisive and action oriented;
- Discipline yourself to take actions immediately
- Practice to make quick decisions
- Remember that unsuccessful people delay decisions, drift throughout life never being happy, complaining, worrying and not knowing exactly what they should do
- Just do it; do not wait for the plan to be perfect.

xx) Never consider the possibility of failure
- It is the fear of failure that paralyze people
- Successful people take calculated risks
- It's not the failure itself but really the fear for failure
- The fact is everyone is afraid of failure but successful people learn to take control of their fear and take action while the unsuccessful people fail to control their fear and avoid taking action.

xxi) Back everything you do with persistence and determination
- Program your subconscious mind to develop empowering beliefs and attitude of mind
- Plan in advance so that you will be persistent and determined
- Persistence is a true measure of belief in yourself and when you have a strong belief in yourself you become unstoppable.

4.3   WINDING UP REMARKS

Remember you are the architect of your destiny and the master of your own fate. Right now you have the potential to accomplish whatever you desire. Remember also that success is predictable,-it is not luck. If you practice these techniques you will have considerable advantage over those who do not. So resolve to use to the maximum your potential and never give up and your success will become unstoppable.

5.0

The Observed Basic Traits Common In All Successful People

Many people have written about the characteristics, the attitudes, habits, pattern of behavior and the important traits of successful people. If you examine carefully they all revolve around the principles of success elaborated above. In this section I have summarized the observable key characteristics of successful people, as explained by 3 writers; i) Stephen R. Covey in his book the "The 7 Habits of Highly Successful People"; ii) Richard St. John in his book "The 8 Traits Successful People Have in Common; and iii) Brian Tracy -"The 6 Habits of Successful People."

5.1   The 7 Habits of Highly Effective People - by Stephen R. Covey

Stephen R. Covey published his book titled *the 7 Habits of Highly Effective People* in 1989 where he elaborated what he considered to be the most effective characteristics of very successful people. The question which is often asked is "are the habits still relevant today?" This question is best answered by the reader of the book himself or herself. What I can confirm, having read the book and compared the 7 habits with the principles of the science of personal achievement is that, they are consistent and indeed very relevant today as it were at the time when the book was written. Just like the 17 principles explained above, the 7 habits will guarantee similar results if they are consistently applied. I am convinced that people who will manage to develop the habits will be able to control fear and a feeling of insecurity, achieve prosperity, avoid the trap and tendency to blame circumstances and the resultant feeling of being victimized and hopelessness, and hence live an enjoyable and balanced life.

From his extensive research and observation Mr. Covey concluded in a nutshell that the most effective people have the following 7 characteristics:-

> ➢ They are proactive;
> ➢ They begin with the end in mind (use power of visualization);
> ➢ They put first things first (they usually ignore trivial/ unimportant things and deal with the important things in the order of priority);
> ➢ They always think win-win;
> ➢ They seek first to understand then to be understood;
> ➢ They synergize; and
> ➢ They sharpen their saw (they improve themselves all the time).

5.2   The 8 Traits Successful People have in Common – by Richard St. Johns

Successful people are not born with the traits that they have in common. They develop them overtime by taking deliberate actions. Overtime they discover the importance and enjoy to do what they do, working really hard, pushing themselves to the maximum, being fascinated with new ideas, improving themselves, serving others and persistence.

They don't inherit the traits from anywhere or sit around thinking about them. They simply apply them as part of their learned behavior or attitude of mind.

Richard St. John, in his book *The 8 Traits Successful People Have in Common,* lists the following:-

> ➤ PASSION: They are passionate about what they do.
> ➤ WORK: They work very hard but at the same time learn to enjoy their work.
> ➤ FOCUS: They focus on one thing at a time and not everything at the same time
> ➤ PUSH: They push themselves out of their comfort zones
> ➤ IDEAS: They consistently come up with new ideas
> ➤ IMPROVE: They keep improving themselves and what they do
> ➤ SERVE: They provide value to others
> ➤ PERSISTENT: They are persistent through hard times, failures and adversities

5.3 The 6 habits of successful People; by Brian Tracy

Brian Trace emphases on developing the right habits arguing that you can learn new habits and you can also unlearn old disempowering habits.

He listed 6 habits of successful people including:-
> ➤ Daily goal setting
> ➤ Being results oriented
> ➤ Staying healthy
> ➤ Being people oriented
> ➤ Staying honest
> ➤ Self –discipline i.e. the ability to make yourself do, what you should do, when you should do it, whether you feel like it or not.

6.0

Do Not Let It Go Untapped

In concluding this Training Seminar Manual I feel excited; I can't wait to see the impact it will bring to the thousands, if not millions, of you who will decide to take it serious, read it through several times, and resolved to apply it towards your dreams. I also hope to see you as participants of my training seminars. In fact, this manual is my guide book for the seminars.

In this manual I have shared my conviction, and the conviction of so many other people who have travelled the same route, that every living person can achieve success. -You see, every one of us has a talent, a gift or a potential which remains within us, waiting to be tapped. If we are able to discover our potential and decide to use it to the maximum, we will find ourselves amazed with the big and positive results we will get. Believe me, I don't have the slightest doubt about this. BUT, unfortunately for many people, it is sad that this will not happen. It will not happen not because they don't have potentials but because they will not take trouble trying to explore them, let along using them. And if they try to explore them they will not mobilize sufficient effort to put them to adequate use. Hence the talents will regrettably lay there idle and only disappear at the end of their journey of life.

I don't want you to get these undesirable results. I don't want you to waste your potential because I am sure your life was meant to contribute something memorable to this generation and generations to follow. I don't want you to waste your lives. Your life has a purpose here on earth. It was meant to leave behind some legacy, irrespective of the size of your contribution. And this is, precisely, the intension of this manual; -to provide you with the necessary package that will make you realize that it is you and only you, who has the power to determine the outcomes of your life. I believe the package contained in this manual is capable of stimulating your inner self, and awaken your slumbering giant, -your little bit of genius within you, to enable yourself to accomplish your dreams and leave a legacy behind.

It is not my intension to summarize the contents of this manual but I would like to point out some few key lessons I consider important as a way of rapping up the manual. The foreword shares with you the five major lessons from my own experience and my long term involvement in poverty reduction initiatives at the national level. These are:- i) The true fight against poverty must be from inside out and not the other way round. As an individual you must resolve, from deep down, and take action, with a strong determination to fight your poverty, come what may. External support will only complement your burning desire and efforts to break your vicious circle of poverty; ii) Blaming external circumstances/forces for failures to accomplish your dreams is merely an alibi. Stop looking for excuses and take full responsibility for everything that is happening in your life, because I can assure you that, external forces, no matter how strong they are, will do very little to push you through, to your dreams; iii) Realize that there are numerous benefits for taking full control of your mind and refusing to allow circumstances to drive you. At the same time, there are penalties that you MUST suffer for neglecting to take full control of your mind and allowing yourself to be driven by external factors; iv) Also take note that for a real and meaningful success, your goals and dreams must not be selfishly focused on yourselves. This is a difficult lesson to understand, but if we really want to achieve more than mere mediocre results, we must make sure that our goals aim to contribute towards improvement of other people's lives; v) the final but most important lesson for your personal achievement is that you should always strive to ensure that your guiding philosophy, mental attitude and beliefs, nurture an empowering winners psychology which is necessary in building your self-confidence and self-esteem. At the same time we must work hard to avoid disempowering philosophy and psychology because it will likewise generate negative results, we do not want.

It is my hope that this training manual has opened up a new way of looking at things and managing your life. I strongly believe and pray that all of you join the 5% group of the most successful people in the world. This is quite possible because all of the ingredients you need to accomplish your dreams are all within you, at the moment. You only need to have big dreams, build up your self-confidence, raise your self-esteem, switch on your inner desire, take massive action and continue sharpening your skills as you move along.

I truly believe that having read the manual to this stage you now have a clearer understanding and appreciation of the distinguishing factors for success and failures in life. You will also by now appreciate the importance and possibly resolve to take full control of your life, set goals and plans, nurture a strong determination and a burning desire and the right mental attitude that will enable you to break all the barriers towards you dreams. The strong determination will propel you to take massive action towards your goals in accordance with your plans.

It is also important to note that, apart from nature, which all of us cannot fully understand, it is only human beings who have the ability to do the miracle of creating new things, from nothing except the ideas in our minds. The ideas and dreams in our minds are the starting point, which must be followed by "actions" to complete the miracle of creation. Mere ideas or even good plans are nothing without the final stage of creation which is actions/activities/work. So resolve to be a person of massive action and personal initiatives.

In this manual I have also shared with you the philosophies of world class Gurus on the science of personal achievement and success. The idea behind sharing the experiences, teachings and writings of the selected few Authorities is to provide you with some guidance towards building your own success philosophies and the empowering winner's psychology. Keep coming back to their philosophies, which is also captured in their numerous inspirational quotes, as you continue your journey towards your dreams. You will feel rejuvenated particularly in those inevitable difficult times when you feel like despairing. For sure there will be difficult and challenging times on your way and to pretend that you can simply wish them away is naïve. At those testing times every one of us normally feel like giving up and indeed many people simply succumb to the challenges and despair. It is at this stage that you will need to appeal to your strong beliefs and applied faith and take advantage of the inspiration we draw from the philosophies of these Gurus.

I have argued that the landmark 17 principles of personal achievement and success by Napoleon Hill, and also those of others included in this manual, are the necessary building blocks for your success. Remember they came out of an extensive research and have been attested by many people that they do work. Indeed they have survived the test of time and more and more people continue to provide positive affirmations to-date. By applying them consistently and persistently successful people have managed to develop such powerful traits and attitudes that guarantee them success for whatever they desire and deserve. I am sure if you decide to apply them, and apply them consistently and persistently, you will also develop strong traits that will make you unstoppable on your way to your dreams.

THE END

References

1. Think and Grow Rich; by Dr. Napoleon Hill
2. Awaken the Giant Within; by Antony Robbins
3. Unlimited Power: The New Science of Personal Achievement; by Antony Robbins
4. Napoleon Hill's Keys to Success: The 17 principles of Personal Achievement
5. The 21 Success Secrets of Self-Made Millionaires; by Brian Tracy
6. The Success Principles: How to Get from Where You Are to Where You Want to Be; by Jack Canfield
7. The 7 Habits of Highly Effective People; by Stephen R. Covey
8. 7 Strategies for Wealth and Happiness with Jim Rohn
9. Foundations for Success; by Jim Rohn
10. Having It All: Achieving your Life's Goals and Dreams; by John Assaraf
11. The Answer; by John Assaraf
12. The Science of Getting Rich; by Wallace D. Wattle
13. Rich Dad Poor Dad; by Robert T. Kiyosaki
14. Rich Dad's Cash flow Quadrant; by Robert T. Kiyosaki
15. Rich Dad's Guide to Investing: What the Rich Invest in, that the Poo and Middle class Do Not!; By Robert T. Kiyosaki
16. Your Erroneous Zones; by Dr. Wayne Dyer
17. Pulling your Own Strings; by Dr. Wayne Dyer

18. How to Live 365 Days a Year: 12 Principles to Make Your Life Richer; by John A. Schindler, M.D.
19. The Success System that Never Fails; by W. Clement Stone
20. The Power of Your Subconscious Mind; by Dr. Joseph Murphy
21. Think your way to Wealth – The lost Classic by the Mastermind of Success; by Napoleon Hill.
22. The Richest Man in Babylon; by George S. Clason
23. The Magic of Thinking Big; by David J. Schwartz
24. Why 2% Succeed and 98% Don't; by John Assaraf
25. The Key to Abundance and Success; by Lisa Nichols
26. See you at the Top; by Zig Ziglar
27. The strangest Secret: How to live the life you Desire; by Earl Nightingale
28. The One-Minute Manager; by Ken Blanchard and Spencer Johnson
29. The Magic of Believing; by Claude Bristol
30. The Power of Positive Thinking; by Dr. Norman Vincent Peale
31. The 8 Traits Successful People Have in Common; by Richard St. John

CPSIA information can be obtained
at www.ICGtesting.com
Printed in the USA
FFOW04n1116050217
32093FF